THE KEY IS LOVE

THE KEY IS LOVE

MY MOTHER'S WISDOM,
A DAUGHTER'S GRATITUDE

Essays to Move Us Forward

MARIE OSMOND
with Marcia Wilkie

 NEW AMERICAN LIBRARY

LT
New American Library
Published by New American Library, a division of
Penguin Group (USA) Inc., 375 Hudson Street,
New York, New York 10014, USA

USA / Canada / UK / Ireland / Australia / New Zealand / India / South Africa / China

Penguin Books Ltd., Registered Offices: 80 Strand, London WC2R 0RL, England
For more information about the Penguin Group visit penguin.com

Published by New American Library,
a division of Penguin Group (USA) Inc.

First Printing, April 2013
1   3   5   7   9   10   8   6   4   2

REGISTERED TRADEMARK—MARCA REGISTRADA

LIBRARY OF CONGRESS CATALOGING-IN-PUBLICATION DATA:

Osmond, Marie, 1959–
The key is love: my mother's wisdom, a daughter's gratitude/
Marie Osmond with Marcia Wilkie.
pages   cm
ISBN 978-0-451-24031-6
1. Osmond, Marie, 1959—Family.   2. Singers—United States—Family relationships.
3. Osmond, Olive.   4. Mothers—United States.   5. Mothers and daughters—United States.
I. Wilkie, Marcia.   II. Title.
ML420.0834K49   2013
782.42164092—dc23   2012050321
[B]

Set in Sabon LT STD Roman
Designed by Alissa Amell

PUBLISHER'S NOTE
Penguin is committed to publishing works of quality and integrity. In that spirit, we are proud
to offer this book to our readers; however the story, the experiences and the words are the
author's alone.
The publisher does not have any control over and does not assume any responsibility for
author or third-party Web sites or their content.

From my heart to those who fill my heart as a mother in every way: Stephen, Jessica, Rachael, Michael, Brandon, Brianna, Matthew, and Abigail. As your grandma would say to me, I will always say to each of you: "I love you more than tongue can tell."

CONTENTS

THE KEY IS LOVE

$\mathscr{I}$NTRODUCTION

My mother loved organization. She even transcribed her handwritten journals into typed pages, dated, and stored in more than twenty-five notebooks.

$\mathcal{C}$harismatic women. Powerful women. Exceptional women. Determined women. Inspiring women. Famous women. In the five decades of my entertainment career, I've worked with many women who are defined by those descriptions.

Starting at the age of three, I was given the rare opportunity to learn some of the success secrets in my world of show business from the top female stars of the day.

To name but a few:

I observed the winning charisma of Pearl Bailey, Cyd Charisse, Kate Smith, Loretta Lynn, Cher, and Dale Evans.

I had an up-close view of the show-stopping power of Ethel Merman, Julie Andrews, Tina Turner, Debbie Reynolds, Dolly Parton, and Connie Stevens.

I absorbed all that I could of the exceptional comedic insight of Lucille Ball, Doris Day, Betty White, Mary Tyler Moore, Ruth Buzzi, Anne Meara, Isabel Sanford, and Minnie Pearl.

I even shared the stage with a new generation of determined and talented performers like Christina Aguilera, Britney Spears, Mariah Carey, and Jessica Simpson.

These are only a small number of the famous females from whom I learned something of value, an idea to contemplate, or a tip that gave me a new perspective on being an entertainer. I was raised to believe that there is always something new that you can learn from the people you work with in every capacity.

Loretta Lynn was a great example for me of a woman who was an award-winning, in-demand entertainment business success story and a loving wife and mother.

Lucille Ball taught me that the best comedy need never be cruel to be funny. She also schooled me on the benefits of good lighting for the female face.

From Pearl Bailey, I learned that giving one's time and energy (she was an ambassador to the United Nations) enriches your performance through life experience.

From Tina Turner, I learned to let the music be an expression of strength and joy.

I could name hundreds more women in all aspects of show business who have graced my life with their groundbreaking individual style and insights into what is, more often than not, a tough career path. There are a few common traits, though. They usually have an intuitive trust in their talent and the personal quality of endurance that gives them the courage and the drive to put themselves out there before the public eye. You have to have that drive because it overrides any lack of confidence. As Minnie Pearl said, "It's the most unglamorous glamour business in the world." She was right. What may appear to many to be a charmed life can also be isolating, emotionally battering, invasive, exhausting, and risky.

Of course, there are incredible rewards, as well. It's an

amazing feeling to be appreciated for what you do and to feel like you have brought happiness to others. I was fortunate that I could observe, in action, some of the best examples of women performers who actually managed to do it successfully.

One woman, though, stands alone as the star who most influenced my life both professionally and personally.

She was the constant light that I could follow without ever fearing I would fall. She was the star who could lead the whole show, but who never took a bow. She never sought the spotlight; but her inner radiance was visible to all who took the time to observe her. In a culture that recognizes a star's power through awards and bigger paychecks, she had neither. She didn't need them. She understood the importance of the part she played in this life. She was never interviewed about an upcoming role, live performance, or album, but the way she acted and the words she spoke made her the perfect role model for me and, I know, for thousands of others. I learned by her example and I succeeded because of her belief in me.

Her last name is on the Hollywood Walk of Fame but not her first. Her first name comes from the ancient Hebrew word *shemesh*, meaning "to be brilliant." As time has passed, I comprehend on a deeper and deeper level how "brilliant" she was. I was named for her, and I pray, every day, that my life will honor that name. She was, is, and will always be my guiding star. She's my mother, Olive Osmond.

For years, I've had a deep and continuous feeling that, as her only daughter, I needed to write down at least some of the countless ways she embodied womanhood and especially motherhood, not only for my brothers and me, but as a woman who truly understood the crucial importance of "mothering" all of God's children, wherever she met them and no matter what their age. She knew the immense importance of her walk in this life as a daughter of a loving God and as a loving mother.

My mother's influence is the core of how I parent my own children and, on a broader scale, how I hope to interact with all my family members, my friends, my fans, and every daily encounter along the way. My mother's philosophy for how to approach every interaction, experience, challenge, and choice in every single day was this: "The key is love." She would always, first, strive to "be positive" and, second, to always be kind. If her kindness was rejected for any reason, my mother's solution was to put forth even more kindness.

I know my daily approach to mothering isn't as consistent or as wise as my mom's, but I also know that she would have been the first one to respond to my shortcomings with kindness and some positive words of encouragement. She was always ready with a positive thought for anyone she would talk to, a thought that would always move us forward in our thinking.

I'm known for saying, "If you're going to laugh about it in the future, you might as well laugh about it now." I even used that phrase for the title of my last book. Like my mother, I believe in a positive outlook on life, but when it comes to motherhood, I feel it's crucial to grasp the seriousness of the long-lasting and far-reaching effects we have on the future through how we nurture our children today. I know it's the single most important "calling" on this earth. A mother is a child's first teacher. We are raising the people who will grow up to influence society and the world. As women, whether we have children or not, we "bear" the future by being the nucleus of the home. There isn't a challenge or a reward in the whole entertainment world that even comes close to the challenges and rewards of motherhood. My mother's generation of women counseled and advised one another over the backyard fence, or in the halls of their church, or at the school bake sale. Considering that 77 percent of women today work outside of the home and more than 30 percent of American homes are headed by single moms, like my own was for four years, we don't really have the opportunities or the time to talk with one another face-to-face anymore.

That's why I want to put on the page some of my own mother's best advice, some of which she noted in her journals, some of which came from her own mother. I noted much of it in my journals over the years. I'm including my own stories of being a mom: the delights, the downfalls, and some of the dreams I've had that you might share in your own parenting.

My mother was charismatic, powerful, exceptional, and determined, though she was never "famous" in a traditional way. However, her influence, like every mother's, will live on generation to generation to generation.

I'm writing about my thoughts as a woman and a mother, most of which are thoughts passed down to me from my mother and her mother before her. My hope in sharing them with you is that they will be thoughts that "move us forward."

Marie Osmond

$\mathcal{I}$F YOU THINK DATING

IS DATED,

DON'T "HANG" AT MY HOUSE

Thousands of fans called her "Mother Osmond." Every week she would receive mailbags full of letters from teenagers asking her advice.

$\mathcal{I}$ think I'll invent an under-eye cover stick for two different times of motherhood. I would call the makeup "2 Weeks and 192 Months." It would have incredible camouflaging capabilities to hide the dark circles resulting from the lack of sleep that a mother has when her baby is two weeks old and again when her baby is 192 months old, which is age sixteen.

When your baby is an infant, being up at two in the morning for overnight feedings is simply what you have to do, a parent's responsibility. You do not have a choice. Your newborn is like an alarm clock going off every two or three hours, day and night, in desperate need of your attention.

When your babies are sixteen, they may not want your attention at all and can go to great lengths to avoid it, but I've found that it's the age when they may need your attention even more.

When your baby is two weeks old, you can't imagine him ever wanting to be in anyone else's arms than yours. At 192 months old, about 90 percent of a teenager's energy goes into thinking about what other arms he could possibly be in, or whose arms might be ignoring him now. However, I've found that asking sixteen-year-olds anything about dating, or whom they might like or who might like them, is pointless anytime before nine p.m. All you'll get is a two- or three-syllable response: " 'S all good" or "Whatever." Then they will find the nearest exit from the room. If you happen to follow them, they will spin on their heels, throw a stop sign hand in the air, and say, "Mom!!!! Really!" After having four kids go through age sixteen already, I've learned not to take this personally.

Like the Cinderella tale, it seems that many sixteen-year-olds don't come back to reality until after the clock strikes midnight. That seems to be the time of day—or night—when they want to process life out loud. Apparently, teens only like to talk about what's on their minds when they are out of the glare of sunlight.

As a mother, I've found that it was a good idea to be up and around at twelve a.m. when their "fantasy ride" is recognized as a pumpkin, and the handsome coachman turns out to have ratlike personality traits. I try to stay up most weekend nights until at least two a.m., listening to whatever my kids need to talk about. I've become more and more nocturnal as more of my kids reached their teen years, mostly so I wouldn't be out of the loop when it came to their relationships. Whenever I could be nonchalantly nearby (if you can call using eyelash glue to hold your exhausted lids open "nonchalant") when my dating teenager was trying to make sense of it all, I'd have the best chance to be debriefed.

I've had to be the breadwinner for my family for the past twenty-five years, like women in 40 percent of U.S. households; and performing five nights a week in my Las Vegas show with Donny means long evenings outside the home. I know I'm not alone in this; many mothers spend long days away from their children. Those children may be in school or day care or watched at home by another adult, but it still comes down to being away from their mothers' love and influence. I know I'm also not the only mother who suffers heart-wrenching guilt about it. As we were running for an elevator after a meeting so I could catch a plane home, a business friend said to me, "I understand your life. I drop my three-year-old off at day care at seven a.m. They take him to his preschool and pick him up. By the time I commute back from work to the day care, it's six fifteen. We get home, eat dinner, I get him in the tub, and he's asleep by eight. I literally see my child for about ninety minutes a day, and it's always when he's tired and I'm tired, too." The pain in her eyes was one I know well. Often my work takes me out of town for shows or business meetings, speeches and appearances. I've tried to make sure that no "travel" job kept me away from my kids for more than seven days. But seven days is a long time in the life of anyone under eighteen. I've had to live with knowing that I've missed out on many of the teenage life issues that my four older kids experienced. I tried to make up for it, but lost time is just that—lost. Both my heart and mind are so much more at ease now in raising my four younger children, knowing that, since my marriage to Steve in 2011, they now have a dependable and loving father who is there for everything that is going on in their lives, especially when I can't be. But it still is painful to me to hear about some of my children's experiences secondhand. Recently, my fifteen-year-old son was arriving home just as I was leaving for work. In the driveway, he said to me, "I don't get to see you very much, but it's okay." Even the fact that he said it was "okay" cut me to the quick. I hid my tears from him, but I cried all the way to work that night.

When one of my daughters was that age, a friend of hers unknowingly made me feel better. The group had gone to see a movie, and they all came into the house around eleven p.m. to pick up their backpacks and other things they had left behind earlier. I was still up, packing for a trip to QVC for my line of designer dolls. All five of them came and sat on the floor of my bedroom to talk. We talked for over an hour about books, music, and video games and eventually more emotional issues: dating, peer pressure, aspirations, and challenges. Afterward, one of the kids said to me, "This was awesome. Sometimes my parents and I don't talk for, like, two weeks. And they would never stay up to talk to me. They always say, 'If it's after ten p.m., don't bug us. We're sleeping.' "

I laughed and said, "Well, I'm sure you don't feel all that chatty when they are wide-awake at six a.m., either, right?"

I guess I'm naturally a night owl, so even if I'm tired, I can manage to find a second . . . or even third . . . wind. It's from a life of doing shows in the evenings and then needing at least a couple of hours for the showtime adrenaline to calm down. My mother was also a night owl, probably from waiting up for us to come home from performing or from our dates. Often in her journals she would note when she felt she could safely relax: *"12:50 a.m. Everyone is under one roof, safe and sound. I can go to bed now."* I'm certain she spent most of her life completely sleep-deprived, but as a child and teenager and even well into my adult years, I never found her too tired to listen to whatever I needed to talk about, no matter what hour of the day or night. I know she was the same way with all eight of my brothers. There are multiple mentions in her journals of getting a post-midnight call from one of her children, even when we were well into our adult years and living on our own.

My mother's wisdom about when we needed mothering the most always trumped any exhaustion she was feeling herself. Her being available to talk to us anytime we needed was a comfort, but it was also a checkpoint for all of us. There was no question of doing anything even somewhat dubious when we were out for an evening as teenagers, because my mother was so present when we got home that it would have been impossible to escape her watchful eyes and ears.

Her favorite creature from the animal kingdom was always an owl, and we all understood why. She was not only wise, but very little went unnoticed when it came to the lives of her children. Like a mystifying plate spinner, my mother could keep all nine of her kids together, but separate, each spinning to his own personality. If one of us started to "tilt" even the slightest, we got a good dose of attention from her. She and my father had a partnership that survived twenty-five consecutive years of teenagers, from the time my oldest brother, Virl, turned thirteen in 1958 to the time Jimmy, the youngest, left his teen years behind in 1983. I sometimes wonder which was tougher: twenty-five years of teenage children or twenty-two consecutive years of changing diapers.

At thirteen, I took a giant step into a new social world in which everyone was at least ten years older than me. This was when the music industry, which was very much a man's world, was acknowledging my first gold record, "Paper Roses." I was Grammy nominated in two different categories, Best New Artist and Best Country Vocal Performance. Here I was, a young kid nominated with Bette Midler, Barry White, Maureen McGovern, Tammy Wynette, Olivia Newton-John, and Roberta Flack. These were artists who had built a career, lived life on their own terms, and had adult social lives as well. Backstage during one of the shows, Sly Stone, of Sly and the Family Stone, invited me to join the party going on in his limousine. I think I mumbled something like, "Thanks, but I can't. My mother and father are standing over there," which I'm guessing got some mileage in Sly's limo later, but he was kind enough not to laugh right in my face. Various show business consultants, managers, publicists, and agents offered advice on which hot, single, up-and-coming actor or singer I should be seen with out on a date in order to get a lot of media attention and boost my career. As exciting as it was to consider the possibilities—and even though by age twelve, I felt like a grown-up—I was nowhere near ready for a romantic relationship! I can thank my mother and father for counseling me and demonstrating to me through their relationship that my goal should be real romance, and not just acting on a passing desire.

Before I lost many of my journals in my house fire in 2005, I had copied something that my mother had handwritten and tucked into my journal when I was a young teenager. This was in the 1970s, a time when previously set standards of social behavior were the target of a lot of ridicule. The TV show *Laugh-In* with Goldie Hawn dancing in a bikini with words and racy images painted all over her body was a giant step away from Sally Field's *Flying Nun*. The "Free Love" sexual revolution of the sixties had set the tone for the seventies. My mother's words gave me a feeling of security and helped me to plot out a map for where my boundaries would be in my dating years. This is what she wrote:

"*Sweetheart, I come from a different era—my mother never spoke of such things. But with the changing times I feel these things need to be said. So how about we don't talk about it, but I will write it.*

"*A young woman should hold herself as a precious jewel. Enjoying life, friends, boys, dating and the opportunity to find life's companion should be a delightful and fun time for you. There are many activities that allow young couples to get to know one another, but dates should never end in physical intimacy. In the sharing of her body with every boy she dates, a girl devalues herself in her own eyes and the eyes of others.*

"*Take time to enjoy the innocence of youth. Kids today are doing everything backwards. They start at the most intimate part of a relationship and then try to become friends after-*

wards. It cannot work this way! All too soon the world will intrude, and life will become complicated with mortgages, bills, jobs, children and all that adulthood encompasses. There is plenty of time to find that one man with whom you feel you want to spend the rest of your life. Do not rush into physical intimacy or it might very well rush you into adulthood before you are emotionally or psychologically capable of handling it. I love you. Love yourself enough to say 'no.' Remember, you might be dating someone else's husband. Mommy"

Now, she wasn't telling me to "Watch out for married men!" even though it might read that way. My mother taught us the Ten Commandments as very young children, and as we became teenagers, she would explain the tenth commandment of "Thou shalt not covet thy neighbor's wife" as a perspective on what we would eventually want in a marriage. She'd say, "Don't you want to feel like 'the only one' for your spouse, to know that you have their unconditional love which can only be built first on a deep friendship and trust?" Rushing into an intimate physical relationship is usually from lust alone and doesn't give you the solid structure of mutual respect that keeps a relationship alive; only time can tell if you have found your true love. "Dating someone else's husband" was her way of telling me that I would only recognize the man who should be my husband if the aspect of physical intimacy wasn't over-riding my heart, if I wasn't confusing lust for love.

When I was nineteen, I met a young man who I thought was the right person for me. He and I were even engaged and making our wedding plans. I had ordered invitations and had decided on my wedding dress. A couple of months into the engagement, I realized that the marriage would have been a mistake for me and that time had given me the grace period to figure that out. But I was worried about telling my parents I wanted to break off the engagement.

I will never forget my mother's reaction when I apologized for already placing orders and prepaying for items that couldn't be returned. She hugged me tightly and said, "That's the best money I ever spent on you! It was an investment in your self-worth. You now know how important you are and why you need the right person in your life."

I thought it was a powerful message that was direct enough for teenagers going through struggles with self-esteem to grasp, and I have repeated it to my own children.

My own daughter was briefly engaged to a young man. She had picked out her wedding dress and was happy and excited for her future. But, just like me, time gave her some insight into the differences between them that she could tell would make the relationship unsustainable. I told her my story and shared the same words of wisdom that her grandma had given me. I was so happy that she had the self-esteem to stick to her values and good judgment. When the time comes, she will give the same advice to her children.

As a mother, the best I can do is teach my children to have self-worth and values, because only these will help them navigate the expectations of our increasingly fast-paced society. My mom always said, "People change, truth doesn't." I've been within earshot of junior high girls talking about their sexual encounters. I know that they think they are so grown-up, in the same way that I did at twelve and thirteen. Yet I can only imagine the emotional turmoil their experiences will create sooner or later, let alone the physical complications and risks.

It's pretty obvious that kids today are under incredible peer pressure for social acceptance that we probably can't even imagine. My parents would switch off the TV if they didn't want us to watch Goldie Hawn dance in a bikini on *Laugh-In*. It's not so simple today. Even the clothing ads at the bus stop and on the home page of Internet servers have images that are sexualized beyond anything that existed in our world thirty years ago.

Teens now even have the constant social pressure that bombards them from their own phones. More than 75 percent of teenagers have cell phones, so it's almost impossible for them to go out on a date to get to know someone, one to one, without everyone in their world also knowing about it. As my high school son tells me, you can't even say hi to a girl in the school hallway without someone texting about it.

It's not easy to keep up with this whole other world of social networking that our kids have grown up with as part of their day-to-day lives. If I have an Internet question about downloading a file, or linking to a site, or even viewing a video, I can usually count on my kids to know how it's done. (Cookies used to be something you baked for someone to be nice!) Even my fourth grader has more computer skills than I do! Our parents might have had to monitor what rock band we wanted to buy tickets to see in concert and what teen magazines were brought in the house, but how can we possibly try to "edit" what our kids are doing on the Internet when we can't even keep up with the technology? Also, according to Nielsen Ratings, the Internet is used by more than 500 million people every week! Really? Imagine our parents having to "check out" who we were spending time with when the possibilities are so overwhelming. One of the guests on my *Marie* talk show who researches usage of the Internet by children put it this way: "Giving a young teenager unsupervised access to the Internet is like giving them the keys to a Jaguar and sending them out on the freeway before they know how to drive."

As a mother, I feel my own particular pressure to try to grasp what my kids are going through, especially since I never had most normal teenage experiences. I never went to a public or private school. I never played a team sport, joined a club, tried out for cheerleader. I didn't get to attend a prom or take a field trip with my peers. I admit that with my older four children, I was often playing "catch-up" with what a typical day at high school was like for them. It appeared to me that their school day consisted of lectures, getting homework assignments, and then returning home to complete them—very different from the way I was educated by a tutor on the set of a TV show or through independent correspondence courses—all this on top of having to memorize 250-page scripts every week for the show or while traveling from concert to concert out on tour.

My teenage challenges were much different from what my own children face. My mom was a very good template for how a woman should treat herself and allow herself to be treated by others. My father was a good role model for my brothers as to how a man should treat a woman because of the way he treated my mother and me. My parents also set strict boundaries on our dating lives. We couldn't date at all before age sixteen and then could only go out on double dates until age eighteen. There were no exceptions to these rules. My mother would tell me that dating one to one would only lead to a physical relationship that we weren't emotionally mature enough to handle. Most of my double dates consisted of one of my brothers and his date occupying the front seat of the car and me and my date in the back, being watched in the rearview mirror. This was not often my idea of a great time, and I think it was intimidating to the poor boys who asked me out and made some of the dates seem awkward at the beginning. Dates were always a structured, planned occasion. Just for a start, the boys I went out with had to have the courage to win over eight protective brothers and parents who kept a watchful eye, and when they rang the doorbell, the person who usually answered was DeVon. DeVon was our bodyguard when we toured and was often around day to day. The best way to describe DeVon is to say that he could have easily been a Samoan NFL player. His neck was the size of my waist, and when he did his laundry, one shirt and one pair of pants filled the washing machine. When I was first allowed to date, I was heartbroken because it seemed that the guys never showed up. I found out several weeks later that my dates fled the scene after DeVon answered the front door in his lava-lava attire and said, "What do you want?" The boys would say, "Is this the Osmond house?" and DeVon would answer, "Do I look like an Osmond?" then proceed to slam the door in their faces! He and my brothers thought this was very amusing.

Double-dating gave me the time to ask myself, "What do you want?" just as DeVon had asked the boys at my front door. I had the time to actually talk to a boy and get to know him because I didn't have to worry about feeling any pressure when it came to physical intimacy. My mother thought it was important for me to date a lot and not make any "going steady" commitments. She advised against dating only one boy. She thought that it would be likely that I would try to become what the boy wanted me to be instead of dating enough to figure out what I wanted in a relationship. I followed her advice. I had a lot of first dates and quite a few second dates. If I had a third date with a boy, that's when my parents started to pay attention. Although this still embarrasses me to admit, as a young teenager, I kept an index card for each boy I went out with in a file box, hidden away in a drawer. On the card, I would describe his hair, his skin, what he wore, and what he talked about. Then I would rate him on his good night kiss. Embarrassing but true. The idea of sorting out my feelings on index cards makes me laugh now, but since I had no sister and no school friends, I didn't have anyone to share my thoughts with about boys. I don't know whatever happened to those file boxes. It's a good thing Facebook and Twitter weren't around in the late seventies. Good to note: Be careful what you write down!

I also learned a lot from group dating when I got an abrupt "wake-up call" from my brother Merrill about being respectful to a boy while out on a date. One evening I double-dated with him and his girlfriend and a boy they had fixed me up with. We started out having dinner at a restaurant. About twenty minutes into the dinner, I knew that this guy was not my type whatsoever. I could barely concentrate on anything he wanted to talk about, and he wasn't at all amused by anything I had to say, either. I decided that his sense of humor had been surgically removed from his personality. After dinner, the four of us were supposed to go on to do some other activity, but I was dreading it, so I pretended that I had a bad migraine and needed to go home.

I thought I had been pretty clever to escape two more hours with him and went on to relish my rare evening alone, doing whatever I wanted on my own time. After working long, long days on the *Donny & Marie* show, just having an evening to myself was wonderful. When Merrill got home later, he knocked on my bedroom door. I could tell that my Oscar-worthy portrayal of "teen girl with bad headache" had not fooled him. I'll never forget him saying, "Your behavior was so disappointing to me. That poor kid. I know he went home feeling terrible about himself. He was really nervous to be around you, and then you wouldn't even stay through the one date he had with you. Bad form, my sister. Do you want guys to say that you're a girl who will stand them up on a date? Don't ever do that again." Suddenly my two hours of free time felt more like a punishment—not from Merrill, but from the truth in his words. I had only paid attention to my own discomfort and not what that boy might have been experiencing. I couldn't escape knowing that I had been selfish to abandon the date.

A couple of days later, I went on a double date with Jay and a girl that he liked and another boy I had never met before. I could tell after the first half hour that I wasn't attracted to this boy, either, but Merrill's words were still playing loudly in my mind. So I decided that I would put some extra effort into being more thoughtful toward this kid. We sat in the backseat as Jay drove us all to get something to eat. As the evening went along, I took the time to ask the boy all about his life, his dreams, and his goals. We talked about music and sports and good movies. I even tried to find some common interests. I knew I wouldn't want to go out with him again, but I had a better appreciation for who he was as a person and the effort it took him to ask me out for the evening. My lesson was learned. It was as my mother had described to me. Dating was about asking questions and using the time to find out who is a good match for you and what qualities you would look for in an eventual life partner. Having a safe way to spend a noncommittal evening was the best way to do this, and so I learned to appreciate my parents' insistence that we double-date until age eighteen.

Of course, this didn't guarantee that the boys I didn't feel interested enough in to see again wouldn't call for a second date. Once again, I learned from my brothers that the way you said no was just as important as being nice on a date. Boys talk to one another about their experiences, too. I know this because I listened to many of my brothers' conversations with their guy friends after they had double-dated. Hearing them talk about the girls they had gone out with was very enlightening when I was younger. It helped me to understand their perspectives and what qualities men look for in a girl.

There are times when it can be a relief for a teenager to have an adult step in and rescue a situation. For a short while, there was a young guy who would repeatedly call to ask me out. I didn't want to see him again, but he didn't seem to comprehend my repeated "I'm busy" answer as a gentle letdown and a hint to give up the pursuit. He continued to call almost every day. One day my mother's frustration at answering the phone yet again made her say to me, with a voice loud enough for him to hear: "Oh, just tell him you can't—your mom said you had to wash your hair!" He never called back!

It wasn't often, but as a girl I really appreciated that my mother would, at times, take the heat for the no I wanted to give when a boy would ask me out. It gave me the freedom to follow my heart without hurting anyone's feelings. I've done the same for my children, especially once they get to the age where they are dating. Even though it's different now—no one ever calls "the house" anymore!—I tell my children to use me as an excuse anytime they feel any discomfort. They have been given my permission to say to anyone, "My mom said no" or "My mother told me that I need to come home now" or "My mother made other plans for the family, and I have to be there." They aren't untruths as far as I'm concerned, because if I sensed any one of my kids felt "stuck" in a social situation they didn't want to be in, I would tell them that I want them to come home immediately. With their flair for the dramatic, a couple of my older kids have been heard saying, "I can't. My mother would ground me for life and then permanently disfigure me." Thanks so much for the great reputation!

Daughters, especially, need a cushion from unwanted attention, without having to be labeled in any way. My two older daughters always told me that I had a sixth sense about it during their teen years. They said that the moment they were being invited to do something questionable, their cell phones would ring and it would be me checking in on them. Jessica told me that it creeped her out how I always rang her number right at that decision-making moment. I had no way of knowing what was going on. I was just following my mother's intuition. It's like a muscle, you know: The more you listen, the stronger it gets. (My mom was Mrs. Universe!)

I think my kids' friends feel, for the most part, that I'm a "fun" mom, because I will laugh and have a good time when they are over to the house. I've even been known to instigate an outing to "TP" the house of a schoolmate; I've mentored them on how a good double roll will have enough weight to fly high over the treetops. (I really should be careful what I write!) However, when it comes to some things, I set very strict boundaries. I've learned to live with being the "unfair" mom, too. When my first four were going through their teen years, I insisted on no sleepovers, ever. Many parents seemed to be fine with the trend of having large coed sleepovers, because as one parent told me, it was "better for us to know where they are."

I could never get on board with that and wouldn't allow my kids to attend, despite some begging and protesting that I was the "only" parent who said no.

Isn't it hard enough to keep an eye on your own teenagers without having to be responsible for ten more kids for twelve hours straight? I also felt I had been given a warning about the possible consequences of coed sleepovers from a young intern who worked on the *Donny & Marie* talk show in 2000. He told me about his high school years and how his parents allowed him to host a big coed sleepover at his house. Even though his parents were both home, in the kitchen fixing food for the gang, one of the girls, upset over being ignored by a boy at the sleepover, got into the medicine cabinet of the parents' bedroom and overdosed on prescription painkillers that the father had for a back injury. The girl fell unconscious, was rushed to the hospital, went into a coma, but eventually recovered. The parents ended up having to handle a lawsuit that lasted for years. I know this is up there in the "worst-case-scenario" category, but I always pay attention to these types of things because I feel that I'm hearing them for a reason. I was told about this incident right as my oldest son and daughter were heading to high school and junior high.

I like mine being the home where my children's friends feel welcome, but it has its limits in their dating years. I think there can be drawbacks to letting teenagers "hang out" together at the house for hours on end, especially if it's a dating situation. Everything becomes too personalized, and both the child and the family lose a sense of privacy. I want my daughters and sons to feel that dating is a special occasion, a fun event. Teenagers' bodies are already raging with hormones, and that's enough to create an unstable situation, physically and emotionally. Having a boy or girl they are interested in "hang" or "chill" and play video games for hours on end in your family room does not teach your children how to build a relationship that has a chance of lasting. As parents, we know that outside of our homes, they are still teenagers, and they don't always make the wisest choices. A lot can happen in a short amount of time. We all have heartache when we see a child get hurt by a poor choice when it comes to dating. That's why I want my own boys to have a moral respect and appreciation for females, and I want my girls to feel that they are special and to know that their self-respect will determine how they will be treated by males. I know it's an old-fashioned perspective, but when I look at the fact that one in four adults ends up living alone, I have to wonder if it isn't a result of the casual disregard that is now prevalent when it comes to dating.

One night after the show, I was talking to a young mother whose daughter was entering the seventh grade that fall. She was concerned about how to protect her daughter's maturity process and to make sure she wasn't confronted with peer pressure in a sexual way that was way beyond her years. She had found this quote on the Internet and shared it with me. The author is unknown, but the wisdom in it is universal:

"We need to teach our daughters the difference between a man who *flatters* her and a man who *compliments* her; a man who *spends money* on her and a man who *invests* in her; a man who views her as *property* and a man who views her *properly*; a man who *lusts* after her and a man who *loves* her; a man who believes *he* is God's gift to women and a man who remembers a *woman* was God's gift to man. And then teach *our sons* to be that kind of man."

When my husband, Steve, came back into my life, we wanted to make sure we took the time to date again. He would ring the doorbell, take me out to dinner and a show, and walk me to the door after our date. I loved it. It made me feel appreciated and honored. It also gave the two of us a structure in which we could talk and enjoy each other's company without any pressure. I'm so grateful that my two younger boys will now have Steve to go to for advice as they move through their teen years.

When each of my boys got to be about eight years old, I would have a once-a-month date night with him. I would have him put on dress pants, a nice shirt, and maybe even a tie, and we would go to a nice restaurant. Then I would teach him to open the car door and the restaurant door and pull out a chair for me; every step of etiquette that my father taught to my brothers, I would teach to my son, from which utensil to use, to folding the napkin, to how to make polite conversation and then listen without interrupting.

When I was on my last book tour, I did an interview with Juju Chang, an anchor and correspondent with *ABC News* and *Nightline*. I told her about my mother-son dates, and as the mom of three little boys, she thought it was a great idea. The next week, she did a video blog about taking her oldest son to a restaurant and got all kinds of positive response.

For me, my father demonstrated how a man should treat a woman of any age; I not only observed how he treated my mother, but how he treated me as a young girl. His appreciation for my mother showed every day in his actions. As I grew up, I thought all men behaved toward women the way my father and brothers did. This is unfortunately not true. I found out the hard way for myself. I would like to think that I could spare my children that costly lesson, but I know it isn't always possible, especially if we don't think we deserve it or it require for ourselves.

To be a human being is to love and to want to connect with others. There are thousands of reasons the adage "love is blind" is so widely known. Many of us have, at least once, been blind in our attraction to someone we thought we knew really well, and ended up finding out that we didn't know them well at all. I think my mother's extremely wise insights about the drawbacks of engaging in physical intimacy before emotional intimacy were solid and true.

It's unfortunate that the word "prude" has such a negative connotation, when after all it comes from the word "prudent," meaning "having good judgment." Being prudent says that you act in a way that shows care for others, for yourself, and for the future.

Of course, the definition of "good judgment" seems to be changing rapidly, even in our school systems. Recently one of my neighbors told me her high-school-aged son came home to tell her that in his sex-ed class, oral sex using a condom is defined as "safe" sex because pregnancy can't occur. Where are we going, as a society, when sex is referred to as being "safe" or "unsafe," instead of being linked with a relationship of love? How can we expect our children to treat themselves and others respectfully when the only question of intimacy is, "Is this safe or not?"

When I was a young woman and we were out on tour, my mother would go with me to the movies. One of the movies we saw was rated GP (the equivalent of PG today) but contained a scene of an obvious one-night stand. Afterward, she remarked, "If the movies treat sexual relations so lightly now, it will only be a matter of time before it is shown on television." She was right. Even today's sitcoms shown during family viewer hours have scenes in which young, unmarried characters are shown in bed together. Why wouldn't this generation of preadolescent kids think that this is a completely acceptable thing to expect in their relationships, even the most casual of relationships? My mother, in her later years, after observing much of this, said the psychological ramifications that occur when there is sex without any commitment, deep intimacy, or connection will destroy a person's self-worth and lead to feelings of being used or objectified.

When you look at the history of societies, being sexually prudent isn't just a moral code of conduct that started with one particular faith. It is life advice passed down through many cultures and religious beliefs. I, personally, was taught that the Ten Commandments were the greatest psychological safety net we would do well to study. Why did God give these commandments? There are long-term ramifications for mental and physical well-being that we all eventually regret if we ignore morals. Many religious texts, honored through time, advise the reader about the negative consequences of physical intimacy just for the sake of physical intimacy. I was fascinated to read that the Kabbalah, ancient Jewish teachings for spiritual growth, holds that there is no such thing as a "one-night stand" when it comes to the effect it has on your soul. What a person might consider a casual sexual encounter may be quickly pushed out of one's thoughts, but it is remembered by the soul. The Kabbalah even suggests that being sexually intimate in a casual manner stays in your energy field or aura for three to seven years.

There are probably hundreds of theories on the psychological significance of intimacy. Women of all ages have talked to me about how hopeless they feel when it comes to having a relationship with a man, especially when physical intimacy preceded getting to really know the other person. I've never met a woman who was truly emotionally immune to feeling regret or to wishing for a more personal relationship, in spite of what the current *Friends with Benefits* types of movies portray as the great life. Interestingly, a LiveScience study from 2008 revealed that young men who had one-night stands felt they had "lowered their standards" regarding their own moral sense of right and wrong for a casual physical experience. Quite a few of the young men who have talked to me about dating tell me some version of "I just want a girlfriend who will be loyal to me, who I can feel emotionally connected with."

Every week I hear from single female friends and fans in their forties and fifties that they would rather be alone than go through one more dating relationship where they feel used and then discarded as the man goes on to his next conquest. What's disheartening to me now is that I see our young women taking on this same "If you don't care, then I don't care" attitude.

I've also had a number of middle-aged single men tell me that they feel that women have become hardened and it's nearly impossible to meet one who doesn't have a lot of anger issues. I think there was wisdom in my mother's sage advice: If the physical supersedes the emotional, then there is no starting point for a true attachment to another person.

In one of the final entries into her journals, before she was no longer able to write, I found this from my mother: "*Women are the moral compass in life. If women lose their self-respect, their beauty, creativity, knowledge, compassion and nurturing qualities, then we will all lose our humanity.*"

What I wish for my own children is that they enjoy their dating years. As my mother wrote to me in my journal: "*All too soon the world will intrude, and life will become complicated with mortgages, bills, jobs, children and all that adulthood encompasses.*" If and when that "adulthood" includes marriage, I want my children to know that they are partnered with a person who is, first, their friend, and second, truly committed to a relationship that will survive all the complications of life—like taking turns when your two-week-old baby wakes you up for a feeding every two hours or your 192-month-old baby makes you lie awake for two hours, waiting for her or him to come home.

The best we can do as parents is to be the example of a

healthy relationship in our own homes. My grandmother never "spoke of such things" to my mother and my mother wrote them in a note to me, then spoke out loud a bit more in her growing concern for the challenges her grandchildren faced in dating in our rapidly redefined social world. Three generations later, in today's world, I think we have to open up the discussion with our kids, probably before junior high school. We need to hear what's going on with them and give them some boundaries, guidelines, and especially encouragement to figure out who they are individually, before they become a pair. And we need to be vocal in our school systems, especially when it comes to teaching about aspects of adulthood that might have a permanent effect on our child's perspective. Practical sex-ed classes don't take moral values into consideration. I've had to make sure my children weren't getting mixed messages. As a parent, that's my responsibility. When I look at the ways my brothers treat their wives and the moral codes they strive to live by, I know that their own children have also learned by example, the same way my brothers and I learned from our parents. I know my own children have been witness to my unhappiness in my past marriage, but they have also watched me make a choice for change. Young children set their moral values according to that of their parents. I hope my life can be an example to my kids of how nothing counts more toward the success of a healthy and happy relationship than abiding respect and a lasting friendship based on the same values. Even when you think your teenagers no longer listen to you, they do. It does sink in. One afternoon I had a "discussion" with my fourteen-year-old daughter about her choice of outfits for a school party because I felt the skirt was too short. It was tough, considering that clothing advertised for teenagers consists mainly of tight dresses with little fabric or short shorts and camisoles. Even prom dresses now have minimal tops and cutouts along the stomach. My son came home from his high school dance recently and said, "I know you expect me to treat girls respectfully, but when they are basically wearing bathing suits to prom, it's hard to know where to look!" I know it's tough on my girls, who want to wear what is current and trendy, like most girls their age. I really do understand. At age fifteen, I had to listen in total disbelief as my mother told award-winning fashion designer Bob Mackie that the clothes he had picked out for my photo shoot weren't "modest enough for a girl her age." I was so embarrassed. I couldn't believe my mother was editing the clothing choices of a top designer. I pretended I needed to use the restroom, and I hid out in there until I was sure my face was no longer red.

As I could have predicted, my fourteen-year-old daughter didn't want to hear that story from her mother's youth! To her, that's ancient history. But later that night, as I happened to be nonchalantly nearby, her twenty-one-year-old sister said to her, "I can't believe I'm actually saying this, but listen to Mom. She's right, especially about dating. If you don't respect yourself, don't expect a boy to respect you, either."

I can hear my mother saying, "Isn't that worth the dark circles under your eyes, no matter how much cover stick you have to apply?"

Purity

A process of freeing ourselves day by day from influences and attachments that keep us from being true to ourselves and to what we know is right. Physical and spiritual cleanliness.

OSMOND FAMILY ARCHIVES

My mother's advice always began with a kind word, which is probably why I still remember it today.

PICTURES TO PROVE

My oldest daughter, Jessica, and me in 2011.

I've got pictures to prove it. Hundreds and hundreds of pictures of my four older children in the pool, playing games, at birthday parties, at school functions, camping, boating, riding bikes and skateboards, gathered around the Christmas tree, eating out together, and on and on. Whenever there was family time, a photo or two were usually taken as well. I remember almost all these occasions with fondness, but when Jessica, my oldest daughter, was a teenager, she was certain that I wasn't present for most of them.

At about age fourteen, she started saying, "You were never there for me, Mom."

Her declarations about my bad mothering skills arose around the same time I was starting to realize for myself that my marriage, following a six-month separation, was not working out. Somehow I rationalized that if I could only find a way to deal with it all that my kids wouldn't have to live without two parents in the home. I didn't want my babies to come from a broken family. No mother does. But even worse, it seemed at that time that my relationship with my daughter might have been permanently damaged as well.

I was absolutely heartbroken to say the least by the thought of losing the affection of one of my kids.

Jessica has always been a very "mothering" child. As soon as she had younger siblings, she became a mini-adult. My oldest son, Stephen, always had his own father, from my first marriage to my husband, Steve, and would go spend quality time with him, which made Jessica the oldest of the children who were living with me full-time. Perhaps it's because she was the oldest, but when it came to organizing the younger brood, Jessica could handle almost any task. She became a mini-mommy.

For example, when I was performing on *Dancing with the Stars* and in the process of getting divorced, I had to be in LA two days during the week. Jessica, who by this time had her own apartment, would come over to the house and get the four younger kids up and through their morning routines, serve them breakfast, pack their lunches, get their homework organized, and drive them off to school and preschool on time. Then she would go to her own job as a media technician, helping to set up for events and parties. Employers always speak well of Jessica because she is a no-fuss, efficient, practical young woman. She is much like her grandma, my mother, and the two of them had a deep and unbreakable connection. My mother was also a very "mothering" child to her younger brother, born when she was in fifth grade. She and Jessica shared a wry sense of humor and a love for a good home-cooked meal. I had always wished that I could communicate with Jessica as well as my mother was able to, especially during those transition years when she was going from a little girl to an adolescent. Even when my mother was hospitalized in the last years of her life after her stroke, she would always hug Jessica to her chest and give her words of praise and encouragement. The most heartbreaking pain for me to see at my mother's funeral was on the face of my oldest daughter. She loved her grandma.

I gave Jessica my middle name as her middle name, Jessica Marie, but for most of her teenage years, I'm sure she would have said that our name was the only thing we had in common. Everything that I am, she seemed to be by nature the opposite. I never leave home without putting on at least some makeup; she thinks a lip balm is plenty. Dressing up makes me feel good; she feels that a shirt that buttons up the front is pretty formal. I would line my shelves with my collectible porcelain dolls; her collection of choice was *Star Wars* figures, *Biker Mice from Mars* figures, GI Joes, and retro T-shirts. (She did have one Betty Boop doll that sat on a motorcycle, a gift from her grandma.) I love to sing; she has a beautiful voice and loves to listen to music but performing isn't anywhere on her list of things to achieve. I almost always run late; she has never missed the beginning of anything, not even a movie, unless she's with me. I'm not the most organized woman on the planet; Jes could tell you where every possession she owns can be found and can often tell me where my stuff is as well. Jessica is technically savvy; I sometimes forget which button on the remote closes the garage door. If I have any technical problems, she is my first phone call. She can usually solve any electronic issue over the phone in forty-five seconds. My day-to-day life moves at such a fast pace, and I meet so many new people every week that I can only concentrate on what needs to happen next. Jessica is more present in the moment, she's reserved with people she doesn't know, and she is always observant, leaving nothing unnoticed.

It's probably this final trait of Jessica's that made me wake up to my true feelings about my marriage. She was not fooled by my attempts to justify staying in it. She knew it wasn't right for me and tried to point it out to me over and over. Even very young children can see to the heart of an issue and often have clear insights into what we, as adults, complicate. In 2010, at age twenty-two, Jessica legally changed her last name to Osmond. Looking back, I can now understand how Jessica could have felt that I wasn't there for her. I couldn't hear her perceptions about the marriage.

I think about my oldest brothers, Virl and Tom, and what a responsibility they must have felt toward seven younger siblings. My parents had expectations of them that I'm certain were more stringent than what Donny, Jimmy, and I experienced. My parents were more at ease with their approach to parenting with the younger set. And let's face it: They were older, too. After the first four kids, you get weary—I know. I get it! The day-to-day routines and self-expectations that all seemed so important with the older children get reprioritized according to your energy supply. There's no doubt that the way I raised my older children is different from the way I am raising my younger four. When in typical teenage fashion, Jessica first started to claim her individuality and push back against the way I thought she should behave, I took it very personally. Now when some prickly, mood-swing behavior bursts out of one of my teenagers, I almost smile about it.

When Jessica was going through her rebellious teenage years, I was convinced she needed a good counselor to straighten out her thinking. (I still think this is a good idea for both children and parents, to have someone who can serve as "referee" when they reach a communication impasse.) I was bewildered that my own daughter was making some irresponsible choices because I would never have "done that to my parents." I couldn't believe she wouldn't even listen to me; I thought I could spare her so much heartache.

I can understand now that she felt her lapses into poor judgment paled in comparison with her mother's choice to stay married when she perceived that I was not happy. I sought out a counselor for us both to see, thinking that it would straighten out Jessica's thinking. It was humbling to hear that it was my thinking that needed an adjustment first.

One afternoon, I went to a follow-up session to talk about the widening gap between my daughter and myself. I was at a loss for what to do. I remember shedding a few tears while I explained to the counselor, "My daughter acts like she can't stand to be around me! I love her to pieces. She thinks I wasn't there for her. It blows me away! I've always taken my kids on the road with me for all of my shows. I've been home as much as I could be, but as an entertainer, I work in the evenings. Why can't she see that I'm trying to support the family?"

The counselor listened politely and then said something

that took me by surprise in its straightforwardness. It even put me off a bit, until I recognized the truth in his words.

"She's a child. You're the adult. Or are you? Picture your daughter as the top of a pyramid. If there is trouble with the child who is at the top, then you have to start looking at the lower levels of the pyramid to see where the problems are coming from—family dynamics, sibling rivalry, your marriage, or even each parent individually. So, take a look at what you are doing that is sending your daughter mixed messages. You're not her friend. You're her parent. She doesn't have to like you right now. She just has to respect you."

I remember sitting there, speechless. I couldn't imagine having a child that I loved so much and so deeply not even like me back. For a moment, my defensive voice roared inside my head, and I sought to justify my position to the counselor, who didn't seem to comprehend the pain I was in. "You have no idea what a mother's love is about! I'm here to heal my relationship with my daughter, and you're saying it doesn't matter that she doesn't like me?" Once my thinking calmed down, after about ten minutes of feeling misunderstood, my heart was able to speak up. "I think he's right. It's almost impossible to love what you don't respect. My daughter needs to respect me first as her mother." It took me a while longer to learn that attempting to justify my position as a parent usually means that my thinking is off base or even incorrect, because hurt pride has replaced true reasoning.

When I looked at myself, and my expectations for her, more closely, I realized that I didn't parent Jessica properly. I wanted her to be my buddy, my friend. I couldn't stand it that she didn't like me. Being a very smart child, she used it to open my eyes to "seeing" the truth I so adamantly avoided.

As I was driving home from that appointment, I thought about another time when seeing things the way others did gave me a new perspective. It happened while touring in Asia with my family when I was a young girl. We were doing a weekend of shows in Bangkok, when the tour manager came up with the idea to give each person in the band and crew a disposable camera on a Saturday morning. We were all given the same instructions. Go out and take pictures of whatever really captures your attention. At the end of the day, all of the cameras were collected and taken to a photo-processing place. (This was before the digital age; you couldn't "tweet" a photo and have it flash around the world. The hippest you could get in the 1970s was a slide projector—and once the lights were dimmed and the fan on the projector began to whirl, everyone in the room would fall asleep!) When the envelopes of photos came back, each person was asked to tape his favorite photos to the backstage wall before the show. It was a fascinating photo editorial of one day from many different perspectives. Some people had taken pictures of clogged city traffic, others of flowering garden walls. There were photos showing street signs, mothers carrying babies, broken-down bicycles, and destitute men on street corners begging for change. There were pictures of lavish temples and cardboard boxes that served as homes to some of the extremely poor, trays full of fish, and trees with colorful flags hanging from them. One of our band members had even taken a picture of some young boy who decided to pee on the American's foot! It was really the first time that I understood how many vastly different points of view individual people can have in the same city, during the same hours of the same day. Even more interesting was that each person thought he had captured the essence of the city best.

I also took the time to think about my own teenage years and how I had felt about my own mother. I occasionally felt hurt that my mother wasn't there for me. I would have long days of rehearsal for the original *Donny & Marie* show surrounded by people who were giving me advice on everything from hairstyles to dance steps to script changes to press photos. Many days I just wanted Mom to be there, at the studio, to guide me in every decision, help me learn my lines, or listen to me when the frustration got to be too much. But even then, I knew it was impossible for her to be there every day, eighteen hours a day, just for me. She had a home to run, businesses to look after, and eight other children who all needed her, too. There are many journal writings by my mother that expressed her frustration at the limitations on her time, like this one from September of 1976: *"I got up at 5:00 this morning to get a head start. I folded some clothes; cooked breakfast . . . and then the panic began. Jimmy's suitcase had been lost, so I had to shorten a pair of pants that he could wear for the taping. We barely made it in time. I'm sitting on the bus (the dressing room at this studio) at KTLA right now watching Donny and Marie on the TV monitor. They're rehearsing an ice-skating segment with Peggy Fleming. I'm doing bookwork at the same time . . . new files, banked checks, paid bills, made reports. I feel so rewarded I don't know how to act! I wish I could be in two places at the same time. I know my efforts could be utilized by each of my kids. I would like to see everything be successful and everyone be happy and have plenty to get along with. Then I'd be happy."* It wasn't until I was married and had my first child that I understood all of the time and energy constraints on a workingwoman who is also a mother. And of course every mother is a workingwoman! You could simply replace the words my mother wrote with your own personal life experience and the frustration is the same for all of us. Once a mother has children, her heart will always be like the ocean, wanting to fill any space where there is a hole, to restore the equilibrium, to make everything equal and fair for every child. As she taught me and I believe with all my heart, "A mother is only as happy as her *least happy* child."

After speaking with that counselor, I had a breakthrough moment of realizing that Jessica's view that I wasn't there for her was *her reality*. It didn't matter how many birthday parties I threw, or how many times I picked her up for lunch from junior high, or how many mother-daughter trips we took, or how often I sat in the bleachers of her sports events; she believed that I was not there for her in her young life. I can understand now why she thought I wasn't there for her, because in reality, I wasn't even there for *myself*. My honest emotions had been buried so deep in trying to be a good mother and keep our family together.

At age seventeen, Jessica told me that she felt she was gay.

She didn't apologize or explain. She just said that she wanted me to know.

Even though I have grown up around many, many gay people in my show business life, and have been friends with them for years and years, it really wasn't something I was expecting to hear from one of my own children. From what I understand, I'm not alone in feeling unprepared for this news. I can't tell you that I didn't cry about it later, because I did. The gay people in my life have told me of the challenges that they have faced simply because they are gay, from bullying to tough workplace discrimination to feeling isolated from social events to legal issues when it came to medical and financial decisions to outright rejection by family members, friends, and even the neighborhoods they live in. I couldn't help but feel saddened at the thought that my daughter might go through similar hardships.

Jessica has suffered from a few broken hearts from what she herself called bad-choice relationships, but many of us have been through the same thing. It seems to be part of the process of figuring out who you are and what your own standards are. She expressed her personality at the time by getting lip piercings and various tattoos. It makes me sad to have any of my babies alter the skin that I think is so perfect, but she was old enough to make that choice. Also, it seemed that everyone was getting tattoos, from rock stars to schoolteachers. It was no longer seen as something radical for a woman to do.

Her younger brother Brandon has always related well to Jessica. He shares her sense of humor, they like the same TV shows, and he always loves whatever clothes Jes picks out for him as birthday or Christmas gifts. Now that she is in her midtwenties, it's wonderful to hear the way she is able to share with him the life experiences that have caused her pain, in hopes that he will avoid them for himself. When Jessica visited to help me get ready for my wedding to Steve, she gave Brandon the type of insight that I now have the time and wisdom to know he probably can't hear from me, as his mother. He was describing to her the tattoo that he couldn't wait to get when he was eighteen. I think Jessica's response surprised him. She told him, "Tattoos give you a stereotype before you even speak. It's like wearing a sign. Unfortunately, people judge you based on your look, so it's really hard to get certain types of jobs when you have tattoos that are visible. It might not be worth it, bud." Jessica now wants to go through the process of having most of her tattoos removed by laser, which is time-consuming and costly, which shows me that she's serious about not wanting them to represent who she is now.

In the fall of 2011, Jessica told me that she wanted to apply for acceptance into the police academy to train to eventually become a police officer. She had decided that her long-term goal was to work with teenagers who were in trouble. I am impressed that my daughter has made her own past troubles into a resource to be used as a bridge to help kids in the future.

Since Jessica chooses to live her life as an "out" gay woman, I've stood by her as a mom who loves her unconditionally. I was fortunate to have a mother who loved each of us unconditionally. I think somewhere in my sweet mother's heart, she knew that Jessica would stand apart from the other grandchildren, at least for a while. My mom's devotion to making sure Jessica knew she was a wonderful girl and loved unconditionally is inspirational for anyone.

Whenever the media has asked me about Jessica's adult life, I always answer that if she ever wants to talk about her personal life, then she will. I grew up in a business where people were always telling me what to do and what to say; I'm not about to do that to my own child. I only want to be there for her. And I hope she knows for certain that I am there for her, always.

Many people have e-mailed me or approached me to thank me for helping them communicate with a family member who is gay. Other times it's a person who wants a bit of encouragement to talk to their family about being gay themselves. I don't feel I have any special wisdom to share! All I can say is that, as a Christian, my understanding of God is that we are each created as one of His own children. I think we need to step back from labeling any of God's children. I certainly don't want my own children labeled and judged with any negative stereotypes about groups of people, because stereotypes never take the individual into account. Being gay is how my daughter perceives her reality. I think all of us can share our thoughts and expand our own thinking, but I don't think we should deny what a person feels is his or her reality.

My mother would tell me, *"Father in Heaven has a relationship with each of His children and there is probably a great counseling place in Heaven where we can one day figure out everything we experienced here in this earth school. In the meantime, let's all love each other. Love is the power that unlocks the door to everything. Love is the key."*

I love my daughter with the same fierce love that I have for my other children. I know this is how Heavenly Father loves us, no matter what circumstances we create for ourselves or have even been put into without choice.

Every day I have to leave the house at about five forty-five to do the *Donny & Marie Show* at the Flamingo. For six months of the year, I commute to Los Angeles every weekday to tape two *Marie* Hallmark talk shows. My younger kids now have their dad, Steve, who helps them through their homework, oversees their chores, picks them up from their activities, talks to them about their problems and accomplishments, and gathers them in the living room for evening Scripture reading and prayers before bedtime. I adore his dedication to being a responsible, loving father. I honor that he looks over each child as if he had done so from the day of their birth. When the younger kids have days off, I take them to LA with me when I'm taping the talk show, and almost every Friday and Saturday night, one of them comes with me to the Flamingo to be with me in my dressing room. However, I imagine that in three or four years a couple of them might say, "You were never there for me, Mom." I'll have to accept that as their truth, no matter how much it is based in reality, or not.

Jessica has always been there for me when I needed her most, especially because I was still a single mom when my son Michael died. Jessica came instantly from Utah to be with the rest of the family in Las Vegas. In those first few days, when I was blind with grief and only able to hug my children and cry, it was Jessica who took over as the efficient and calming maternal presence. She got breakfast and lunch for the younger kids every day, made sure they cleaned up their rooms, brushed their hair, and put on clean clothes. She helped make sure the house was kept in order and organized the flowers and food that came to the front door. She threw in loads of laundry. She stayed up late and got up early and listened to every emotion that any of the younger kids wanted to express, denying her personal need to grieve until later.

Whatever Jessica and I have been through as family, I know that we were always meant to be mother and daughter. From the moment the social worker in California called me to come for my new baby girl and the nurse put her in my arms, I knew she was mine. In fact, right before that happened, the nurse had accidentally pointed me to another bassinet, holding someone else's infant. As adorable as that baby was, I somehow felt strongly that a mistake had been made. Moments later, apologizing profusely, the nurse told me that my baby was in a different room, apart from the regular nursery. And there she was, the child whose face I had envisioned in my thoughts and prayers. I had even described her in my journal long before she came into my life. Finding my daughter in a "different room" has always been a bit of a humorous metaphor for our whole relationship. We aren't always in the same "room" as far as how we each think, but we will always be mother and daughter, and that bond is unbreakable.

As parents, many of us believe that it is our responsibility to teach our children, but I've found we are also here to learn from these special spirits that we have been blessed to raise. When it came to parenting, my sweet mother would tell me, *"It's like an hourglass on a table. You think that you have put in the time and that you have it all figured out now. And then the hourglass gets turned over by something unexpected or a life change and you find yourself having to learn more patience and grow even more as a mother."* Like sand through the hourglass . . . these are the days of our parenting lives!

The best we can do as parents is to teach and lead by example, then stand aside as our children learn to govern themselves. Through our unconditional love we need to support them, even if their personal beliefs are in conflict with our beliefs about what is best for them.

On one of Jessica's recent visits, she sat next to me for a while as I scrolled through hundreds of family photos on my laptop to choose some for a school project for my youngest son. I realized that I really wasn't in many of them. It was hard for me to find candid photos of me with my kids.

I said to Jessica, "I can see why you thought I was never there for you. There are hardly any pictures of family events with me in them."

When she turned to look at me, there was not a single ounce of triumph in her eyes. "You were a working mother," Jessica said. "You did the best you could. Besides, you were there. I remember it."

I turned to look at my adult daughter, who is now, thanks to time, effort, and healing, also my friend. "You do?" I asked.

"Yes, Mom. You were always the person taking the picture."

Dignity

Honoring the worth of all people, including ourselves, and treating everyone with respect.

Happy to be sandwiched between two incredibly strong women: my mother, Olive May, and my daughter, Jessica Marie.

BREATHING IN AND
BREATHING OUT

My family just months before my brothers stepped into the spot-light on the Andy Williams Show: *(clockwise from left) Jay, Alan, Tom, Virl, Wayne, Father, Donny, Merrill, Mother, and me. Jimmy would join the family a year later.*

$\mathcal{M}$y oldest brother wasn't "brought by the stork," but he was carried around like he was, at least the first couple of days of his life.

My mother, who was just twenty, had almost no prior experience with babies. She had been an only child for ten years until her baby brother came along. She wrote in her journal, about her firstborn, Virl: *"I didn't even know how to pick him up properly. I was so afraid of hurting him or kinking his little neck. I would wrap the blanket real tight around him and then pick him up, holding the blanket with both hands, one over his chest and one over his knees."*

My father told me how my mother would gather the corners of the blanket and carry the baby as if in a sling. When the nurses would come in to change him, my mother was terrified by how swiftly they handled her infant and would cry out, "Please don't drop him!" This was back in the mid-1940s when a woman stayed in the hospital for almost two weeks after she had had a baby. How much wiser was that than our current hospital policy of sending new mothers home twenty-four hours after delivery? It makes me wonder if so many reported cases of extreme baby blues, postpartum depression, and even infant illnesses could be prevented if the mother was given time to recover and rest for a few more days, and learn to care for her baby while she is being cared for herself.

Thankfully, my mother's roommate in the hospital was a woman who had just given birth to her fifth child. She may have been secretly very amused by my young mother's first-time nerves, but my mother remembered her as being kind and helpful and answering her string of questions about raising children. One of the first things the experienced roommate told my mother was "Babies aren't all that fragile."

Perhaps babies aren't all that fragile, but new mothers are. It doesn't seem to matter if a woman becomes a mom for the first time at twenty or thirty-four or forty-two—there is an undeniable shift in perspective and priorities that leaves you feeling as if you are permanently relocated to a brand-new world. You are, within hours, a woman who now holds in your arms another life that is completely dependent upon you for everything. It probably wouldn't be so overwhelming if the baby could at least talk and verbalize his needs. But I understand God's wisdom in having that *not* be the case. New mothers want to fall in love with their babies, and even though infants cry, it would be a whole other story if they could verbally complain right out of the gate. Can you imagine your newborn saying, "Really? *Ducks* on my blanket? Hello! I'm going to be a dog person."

When my mother went home from the hospital, she put her newborn's bassinet right next to her bed so she could hear him all night long, breathing in and breathing out. She was end-lessly concerned about *"a rattle sound"* in Virl's throat, which the pediatricians told her was normal. All night long she would jump to her feet at his slightest whimper to see what her baby needed.

I'm not sure my mother ever got another good night's sleep until 1981, when my brother Jimmy, her last child, turned nineteen and my parents went on a church mission to Hawaii. Actually, by then she usually had one or two or seventeen of the grandbabies around, so any slumber lasting more than a couple of hours was a very, very distant memory.

In a journal entry from November of 1945, my mother wrote about rocking her baby for hours at night while reading *Parents* magazine or anything she could find to *"make me be a good mother."*

I have a hard time envisioning my mom feeling uneasy about her caretaking skills. She had an ease and confidence by the time I came on the scene, but I can tell by the entries in her journals that she worried constantly as a first-time mother.

I had never felt a bigger sense of accomplishment than when I gave birth to my firstborn at age twenty-three. No chart-topping single, or hit TV show, or part in a movie had ever made me feel that I was a part of creating something wonderful more than holding my newborn son for the first time. I dissolved my sense of self into his spirit, and his link to me was, and still is, unbreakable. I felt the calm that comes with know-ing what the purpose of life is about. I wanted to suspend that feeling into eternity.

Like my mother, though I didn't know it then, I was a fragile first-time mom, not physically, but emotionally. Giving birth to my son replaced the "Marie Osmond" that I had come to accept as me, and left me feeling vulnerable when I thought of what the future would hold. I had spent years learning how to have "stage legs," as they say, but wasn't as confident about having "mommy arms."

All of the facets of my career life that I had so carefully monitored before, like weight, fashion, concert tour schedules, photo shoots, press appearances, and more became diminished in importance by things like a baby monitor. It was a terrifying transition for me, but I went forward with enthusiastic naïveté until I became utterly depleted. I was exhausted by my own expectations.

When you are a first-time mom, I think you want to believe that there is a "right" way and a "wrong" way to take care of a child's needs, until you gradually begin to understand how unpredictable being a parent can be. I was used to growing up in the entertainment business, where you rehearsed until you got it right and then, and *only then*, did you present it to other people. With a baby, there was no rehearsal, so I became preoccupied with making sure everything was "right" from the start, from sterilizing everything until it almost melted, to daily bleaching the burp cloths and bibs, to every baby accessory a nursery could possibly hold, to making certain his little outfit matched from head to toe with a coordinating blanket and hat. Also, like my mother before me, I had to have my baby right next to me at all times so that I could hear him breathing in and breathing out. I would hold him in my arms for hours on end and would only sleep if he could be nearby. This was true for each of my babies. I could only rest myself if they were within arm's reach.

In theory, it all sounded good. But what it meant in practicality was the extreme opposite. If my infant's pacifier dropped into the car seat momentarily, then I'd have to choose between a possible germ that might have clung to it or a wailing son for the next fifteen miles. Using a burp cloth only once meant a huge stack of laundry by the end of the day. Also, if some spit-up landed on his blanket, then my only option was changing his entire outfit as well to maintain my "coordinates" plan.

About a month into being a mom, I fully understood that my "bundle of joy" was also a "pack of projectile *everything*," and the beautiful "mother and child" image that I had always pictured in my head was now wet-wiped with reality.

I used to wonder why my mother never told me the "truth" about being a first-time mom. When I was certain I could be a perfect mother, she would smile and nod and say something like "I'm sure you'll do fine." She never tried to talk me out of my expectations, even though her own knowledge of taking care of a newborn was so great she could have written a baby book.

I know now that she wanted me to have the experience fully for myself. She must have known that in time I would replace the idea of being "perfect" with the idea of being "present" and bonding with my baby. After nine kids, my mother knew good and well that "babies aren't all that fragile" and that he would be fine through all of my "rehearsals."

One of the very few times I saw my mother weep in a fragile way was when her own mother passed away. I was a young teenager then and was in my room at home, suffering my own sadness at the loss of my grandmother. When my mother came in to check on me, she sat down on the edge of my bed to talk. I am certain she didn't expect what happened next. Overcome by grief, she dropped her face into her hands and cried, "Now who will take care of me?"

I was frightened by her emotion; I had never known my mother to be anything but a stable force in our home. The only tears I had seen her cry before this were tears of joy or at least warmth at an uplifting story. Watching my mother weep from heartbreak was something I never forgot and only understood more deeply as my mother aged.

No, "babies aren't all that fragile," but new mothers are, middle-aged mothers can be at times, and, inevitably, old mothers become fragile. As I said, it doesn't matter at what age a woman has her first child, the newness of the experience is still the same. I now know that the same is true in reverse. It doesn't matter at what age a woman loses her mother—the loss of that first and most significant relationship is the same.

When my mother had her massive stroke in the fall of 2002, at age seventy-seven, she was airlifted from St. George, Utah, where she and my father were living, to a hospital in Provo, Utah, which had the specialized surgeons to deal with her bleeding aneurysm.

My brothers flew in from around the country to join me at my mother's side as the medical team explained the risks of performing surgery. She could have died on the operating table, and should she survive, her chances of full recovery were slim.

My brothers, father, and I came together in prayer. We asked for guidance for the surgeon, doctors, and nurses who would be attending our mother. Afterward, our father opened the Scriptures to a verse that gave us comfort, which said in essence to let God be God. We prayed for whatever God's will would be in our lives and in our mother's life.

After her surgery, I felt strongly that my mother's will to live was in agreement with God's will. I think she knew she had one more way to help us to grow in understanding and appreciate the cycle of life, and that was to show us the grace involved in departing this life.

My mother never did recover her ability to walk or even speak with her full voice. She was in a rehabilitation hospital for over a year, after which we relocated her to a new home that was much closer to her doctors. We had nurses come in to take care of everything medical, as she now needed a machine for oxygen and another for feeding, and various IV lines.

This coincided with the time in my own life when my last child, Abigail, was heading into the terrible twos, old enough for me to go back to work full-time, even if that meant travel. Broadway had beckoned to give me a lead in a musical. Hollywood was calling to see if I was interested in various shows. Concert promoters were asking if I planned to tour. I could have gone. Virl was at hand every day to help my parents, and Donny and his wife, Debbie, lived in Provo as well. My mother would have told me to go on with my career, but my heart told me to stay.

I wanted to be near my mother. I needed to participate in her care, from the complicated duties of keeping track of medical information to the simplest care, like brushing her hair and rubbing lotion into her arms. I wanted to get her opinions on the new dolls I had designed for my next Marie Osmond series and take the time to paint a gorgeous border of climbing roses along the top of the walls of her room with the help of my lifelong friend Patty. My mother could no longer sit at a sewing machine, like she loved doing, so she watched as I made her pretty nightgowns and designed a new quilt. I wanted to comfort her and make her smile. I wanted my children to have that time to be with her. I wanted to be even closer to her so that I could hear her whispers of wisdom about all aspects of life: from keeping house, to keeping peace at home, to the peace she felt as she prepared to go back to her "heavenly home."

One morning, after dropping my children off at school, I stopped in to see my mother. She seemed to be in pain from having to be turned onto her side for a treatment. She winced at the effort it took her to move her legs even a little. After it was over, I lay on the hospital bed next to her.

"Mommy, I know how hard this is for you," I said, patting her arm. "I'm so sorry you're suffering."

She smiled and motioned for me to get her pencil and paper. I put the pencil in her hand and held the pad up. She struggled to write down six words. When I read them, tears fell from my eyes. She had written, "I love every breath I take."

Over the next six months, I helped stand watch over her as she became more like an infant, completely dependent, unable to speak and sleeping for hours and hours on end.

In the months before she left us, there were two occasions when my brothers and I thought the hour was at hand. At those times, Virl would be there around the clock to support my father. My brothers would, once again, fly in from around the country, and we would gather, as a family, in her room. Once we were all together and talking and sharing our lives, she would somehow stabilize and continue on. My brothers and I would look at one another knowingly and laugh. Our mother just wanted to make certain that we all stayed close through this time.

At two a.m. one night, I sat alone in her room, trying to knit a scarf for my daughter. My heart was grieving that I would soon be a motherless child. However, my spirit was peaceful, knowing that I had answered my mother's question of years and years before: "Who will take care of me?"

"I will, Mother," I thought to myself. "I will and your beloved firstborn son, Virl, will and all of your other sons, too. In the same way you selflessly cared for us, all of your precious children will be here for you: Tom, Alan, Wayne, Merrill, Jay, Donny and Jimmy. And, I know, in time, your grandchildren will take care of your sons and me, when our life cycles come to a close."

I wanted to suspend that feeling of peace into eternity, as I sat there listening to the gentle rattle of my mother breathing in and breathing out.

Service

Doing helpful things that make a difference to others. Investing excellence in everything we do. The contribution we make is the fruitage of our lives.

You've got to hand it to the creator

My third child, my sweet daughter, Rachael. My mother took a twelve-hour flight to be there for her arrival.

OSMOND FAMILY ARCHIVES

On a page of my journal from November 2002, there is a simple drawing of one moment in time. A few weeks or months later, this exact drawing could have never been made, because the subject would change so much. The image was drawn using one continuous line and took no artistic talent at all; it was only a matter of tracing around my child's hand on the paper. Next to the handprint I wrote, "Matthew, age two and a half." This was one of the few journals that survived the house fire in 2005 that destroyed my home office and most of my personal collectibles, scrapbooks of the children, treasures passed down from my grandmothers and mother, and many of my journals.

I do most of my journal writing late at night, or in the very early morning, depending on your perspective. Not only is there the least possibility of an interruption, but the peace and quiet allows me to hear the soft voice of intuition, or what I call "downloading my spiritual feelings." Postmidnight is when my mother did most of her writing, as well. In one of her journals from May 1975, when we were performing in Paris, my mom wrote: *"I'm tired but don't want to go to bed. I guess I'm a night person. I love the quiet, peaceful time of evening when I know my family is safely tucked in bed. Then I can read, write, file ideas quietly and concentrate."* I understand her writing this. I smile as I glance over at my clock to see that I am writing this chapter at two o'clock in the morning.

During the day, mothers just have to trust that our kids are out there in the world, every day, and we hope doing okay. But at night, all under one roof, you can have the peace of mind of actually knowing where everyone is, and for a few hours, your mind doesn't have to wonder if they're safe. Even now, when my older kids are visiting and go out for an evening together, I have them come tell me when they're back home for the night. They always laugh at me and say something like "You never know when we're out the rest of the time," which is true. But like other moms I know, I find it hard to sleep because you always listen for them to come home.

Over the years, whenever one of my kids was up in the middle of the night because of a bad dream or a tummy ache, I would take their minds off their upset by tracing his hand onto a page of my journal. If I still had all of my journals, I'm sure there would be half a dozen handprint tracings of every child.

It's hard to believe that this tiny handprint from 2002, which filled only half of a six-inch-by-nine-inch journal page, belongs to my youngest son, now a thirteen-year-old with long, thin fingers and hands that are bigger than my husband's, strong enough to hurl a football dozens of yards and reach every key on a full-size saxophone. He is taller than I am even in my heels. The suit I bought for him to wear to church six months ago and had altered to fit him perfectly already needs to be given away, unless capri pants come into style for boys' suits. The other day, when I picked him up to go to the orthodontist office, I didn't recognize him waiting in the school parking lot. The cells in his body are dividing and multiplying faster than the interest rate on the credit card I use to buy him new clothes every ninety days. Late at night, coming home from doing a show, when I trip in the dark hallway over the size eleven-and-a-half sneaker he left at the top of the stairs, I try to remind myself that this tugboat of a shoe with forty-two inches of mud-caked laces represents the tiny foot that kept me awake at three in the morning, internally wedged between my ribs, kicking at the base of my lungs until I gasped for breath. This shoe belongs to the miracle of God's creation: a child.

A few weeks ago, I received an e-mail from a friend's daughter that contained the 3-D ultrasound image from her twenty-two-week pregnancy, her developing child's first public portrait. This young woman was able to see the miracle of God's creation as it was happening. Pregnant women today have the option of viewing their baby from every angle, a definite fast-forward in modern technology, even in the last decade.

In the 1920s, when my grandmothers were pregnant with their babies, they had no choice but to carry on through the nine months in a trusting faith that everything was fine with the life growing inside of them. Being under a doctor's care and supervision was financially impossible for either of my grandmothers, as it was for most women of that time. My parents were both born at home with only the help of their own grandmothers and perhaps a midwife.

In 2010, our family was honored by a generous group of donors, who restored the tiny two-room log cabin in Malad, Idaho, in which my mother was born and lived for the first years of her life. It's now a small museum, displaying items from her young life, including her first sewing machine and the cabinet that my brothers carved their initials into as little boys. I contributed quilts she had sewn over the years and, of course, dolls from her collection.

Today, women who are expecting have access to expert prenatal care developed from decades of research. And on a day-to-day basis most women have Internet access to almost any kind of information about pregnancy that we could possibly need. There are classes taught in making the actual birth process as stress-free as possible and available support for every step of the way. Once your infant arrives, there is every creative baby accessory that any new mother could hope for available at the nearest mall. It's easy to underestimate the hardships of generations of mothers before us. My mother used to chuckle about all the accessories young moms seem to find it impossible to do without today. When she raised us, she made do with a bassinet, a crib, a high chair, and a blanket on the floor for us to play on. Our baby bathtub was the kitchen sink, our changing table was the dresser top, and our car seats were whatever adults could hold us tightly on their laps. The only Diaper Genie she knew was a farm pail and some water with bleach that she put the soiled diapers in until she could put them in the washing machine and then hang them on the clothesline outside to dry. My mother thought disposable diapers, when they came along, were the invention of the century (although later she would rethink her position and say that disposable diapers were too much of an expense, a lot of extra waste, and hard on babies' tender skin!).

In my mother's journal from 1951, she wrote of her overwhelming gratitude when, pregnant with her fourth child, her neighbors gave her a baby shower: *"I had never had a baby shower and felt a little uneasy about it—having people bring me gifts. I never had a birthday party when I was a kid, either. We were quite poor and my parents just didn't think it was right to have parties and have people bring gifts—especially since Dad was a teacher in the community. I understood their thinking. Anyway, I didn't have anything to say about the baby shower. The party had been planned and a lot of friends had been invited. It was so fun and I got several beautiful little baby dresses. Everyone thought since I'd had three boys I was sure to get a girl this time. I so appreciated their thoughtfulness."*

Her journal entry in late August that year speaks of her pure joy over boy number four.

"Our dear little son, Melvin Wayne, was born at the hospital in Ogden, Utah. I was so thrilled that he was strong and I could hold him in my arms."

And even though she wouldn't be able to use the baby dresses for eight more years, I was amused to read about how obviously excited she was to have a baby that didn't look exactly like my dad.

"He weighed 7 lbs and 3 oz and had a different look than the other three boys—and I was delighted—because he looked more like me! My childhood pictures surely proved that."

My mother gave birth to all nine of her babies over the years in various hospitals, and not once did she know ahead of time what gender her baby would be or if the infant would be healthy or have any clue what each of us would look like.

Not so anymore.

Near the end of my second pregnancy, my parents were both serving on a church mission in London. I was feeling tired and experiencing some cramping, and so I was lying on the couch when my mother called me in Utah. She asked how I was feeling, and I told her I was fine, just tired, because the baby was due in the next two weeks. I also told her how much my ankles and legs had been swelling in my last trimester. We chatted for a while, and I told her I would call her in a week or so. Well, about four hours later, I went into an unexpected early labor. Before I left for the hospital, I called my parents and my father picked up the phone. I had barely spoken before he told me, "Your mother left for the airport three hours ago. She's on her way there to be with you." Somehow, my mother's maternal intuition told her I would be needing her by the end of that day. Was she ever right.

Once I got to the hospital, they began to monitor the baby

and realized the heart rate was elevated quite a bit with every contraction. Around the time my mother arrived, they decided to do a sonogram to see exactly what was going on. I was naturally anxious to have the doctor look at the image and tell me that everything was in perfect order. My mother had absolute faith that this baby would be a *perfect* blessing from God, no matter what the sonogram revealed. She believed that every single child is perfect, no matter how science would weigh in on the matter, and having my mom there to remind me of that was a great blessing to me.

My mother poised herself on the edge of her chair, notebook and pen in hand, as the technician described how the high-pitched sound waves in a sonogram bounce back an image onto the screen of what is going on in the mother's womb. I had to smile as my mother took voracious shorthand notes of every detail of the process. At one point, the technician laughed and said, "Don't worry, Mrs. Osmond. You're not going to be tested on this information." As the daughter of a schoolteacher, my mother never passed on the chance to learn something new. It didn't seem to matter if it pertained directly to her life or not. She loved to have new information and enjoyed passing it along to others; I know she passed her endless curiosity and limitless love of learning on to me.

We were both speechless when we saw the image of the next Osmond grandchild on the screen. The doctor pointed out that I had an excess of amniotic fluid and that my little daughter was literally swimming laps in my belly. They felt it was important to take the baby out because she was already nine pounds and there was more danger to deliver her naturally as the umbilical cord had wrapped around her leg, stressing her heart with every contraction. All in all, she was healthy and strong. There were no words, even in shorthand, to fully describe the miracle before our eyes. She almost seemed to be smiling at us as if to say, "I was just passing time until Grandma got here."

As the top of her head crowned, they put wire electrodes on her scalp to monitor her heart as she came through the birthing canal, which stunned my mom. When the doctor saw it was becoming too much for the baby to handle, he used a suctioning device to pull her out quickly. It was like a giant plunger that left her flexible skull a little bit pointed for a short while. My mom, who could find humor in any situation, lightened any stress in the room by saying, "She looks like a conehead child." The attending doctor and nurses all burst into laughter, never expecting a comment like that from an adoring grandmother.

Years later, when I went for my sonogram during my final pregnancy, my oldest son, Stephen, who was then sixteen, went with me. About six months before I became pregnant, I had mentioned to the older children that I had a deep inner feeling that our family was supposed to have one more boy. Stephen, who already had five younger siblings to deal with, two of them under age three, probably felt that, when it came to my feelings on having more children, I should maybe tell my inner voice to zip it. When, against the odds, I ended up pregnant at age thirty-nine, Stephen just shook his head in amazement.

I was amazed that he wanted to go with me to my twenty-week ultrasound, but I thought it was really sweet of him: the oldest who couldn't wait to welcome the youngest. I didn't realize his true motivation.

During the appointment, we were both in silent awe as we watched the image appear on the screen. Stephen sat silently as the medical assistant moved the wand across my stomach, displaying the baby's head and arms. Then he piped up, "Let's get to the important part here. This better be a boy, or knowing my mom, we are going to have one more kid in the family besides this one."

Little did he know then how true his prediction would be!

To me, a baby is proof that all of creation is in God's hands and that we should always hold hope for the future, even though we won't ever know what the future might hold.

Human beings may have the intellectual skill to invent an ultrasound device that can view a fetus in the womb and detect the flicker of a heartbeat before a woman even knows she is pregnant, but no one has ever determined how a human being gets created in a very distinct order. Any scientist can explain how the zygote comes to be from the egg and the sperm and can even give a detailed account of how cells divide and multiply. Yet no scientist has the explanation for how one cell becomes the baby's cornea and another cell becomes the spleen, while another forms the heart as another becomes the spinal cord.

The process of growing a baby remains untouchable in its perfect order. There has never been a "new and improved" version of becoming a human being. Nothing that comes in a Tiffany blue box or on a canvas in the Metropolitan Museum of Art or is engineered by Mercedes-Benz perfection can equal the beauty, design, and miraculous order of creating a human life.

My mother felt the same way and noted on a journal page after one of my brothers' births: *"There is no thrill in this world that can equal that of having a child."*

I believe that it is the way the Creator delineated the genders from the beginning of time: To the male was given the seed and the potential to create; to the female He gave the ability to nurture that potential into a reality. The women in my long family line have believed for centuries that there is no greater calling than being a mother, nothing more important to the continuation of life. I include every female who carries a pregnancy to full term, even if she knows it's not her child to bring up.

I write these words as a grateful adoptive mother. I can understand that, even though a woman has the potential to create a new life, she may not be ready to raise a child, or even feel that the fetus she carries is connected to her in a mother-child relationship. Yet in her pregnancy and through adoption, her ability to bring the joy of motherhood to another woman is infinite.

For my mother, a woman's "choice" was whether she wanted to have sexual relations with a man, but if she did conceive, my mother felt it was no longer just the woman's choice because now there was another life involved. My mother was adamant that abortion was only to be considered in a case of rape or incest, but even then it should be a decision handled with much prayer and fasting. She wrote in one of her journals from the early eighties: "*Abortion should never be used as a form of contraception. That's rationalization and justification on the part of a woman's thinking.*" She didn't surrender her opinion even when it became more controversial. She based her belief on what she learned from reading and pondering the Scriptures, which she also noted in her writings: "*As thou knowest not what is the way of the spirit, nor how the bones do grow in the womb of her that is with child, even so thou knowest not the works of God who maketh all*"(Ecclesiastes 11:5). Her love of all people and her willingness to defend the precious gift of life is one of her "thoughts to move us forward."

My girlfriend Patty, who grew up with me and knew my mother most of her life, said to me after reading this quote from my mother's journal, "Isn't it odd that our society is so fascinated by the idea of finding life on another planet, yet we don't even honor the life that is on our own?"

In the 1950s and early 1960s, when there was quite a stigma attached to pregnancy out of wedlock, my parents made room in their growing household a number of times to give shelter to young women who found out that they were unexpectedly pregnant. Each young woman would live with us for four or five months, helping my mother take care of her growing family and the household. At the same time, my mother would "mother" her, giving her encouragement, cooking, sewing, and budgeting skills and subtle lessons in self-esteem and finding their life path. Most of the young women left my parents' home feeling that they had fulfilled a grand purpose by bringing a child into the world, some who would be adopted and raised by loving couples longing to be parents and some who would remain with the young mothers, now ready to love and embrace the babies as theirs. My mother would never support the thought of the young woman making a choice about her baby under any pressure from anyone. She would always encourage them to pray, listen to their intuition, and then follow it. She believed that was the way that a young woman could find peace with her decision, even when the decision was a tough one, or despite whatever challenges she would face in the future. Making a decision from fear will only lead to regret or sorrow. Peace of mind and heart will grow and then sustain a woman's decision through the years.

Once on the *Donny & Marie* talk show, we did a full hour on adoption, with special guests including both birth mothers who had given their babies at birth and the loving couples who had adopted their infants. (I prefer to not link the words "given up" even though that term is so generally accepted for the choice a birth mom makes. After all, this infant is such a gift to the mother waiting for him or her, and a gift is given, not "given up.") The birth mothers on this show were in their late teens at the time of their pregnancies, and yet they seemed to have an old-soul wisdom about the best outcome of their pregnancies. Each reported feeling strongly that the baby had real parents who were waiting for him or her, and that their part in this natural transition was to bring that child into the world for them. The obvious happiness of the adoptive parents holding their long-awaited children brought the audience to tears.

The reality that some of my children were created from the zygotes of other women and men, most of whom I never knew, only increases my awe at the miracle of creation, especially since I knew that each child was mine even before he was born, and I felt the mother-child bond from the moment that baby was put into my arms. I know I'm not alone in this. Other adoptive mothers have told me the same thing, including Valerie Harper, Donna Mills, Teri Garr, and Sheryl Crow, along with many of my personal friends.

In one of my mother's early journals she describes the miracle of holding her firstborn in her arms for the first time: *"As they laid him in my arms, I continued to weep with joy, knowing that this dear little life was mine. I was actually his mother! How I loved him. I was the happiest person in the whole world. It was truly the most profound moment of my life."*

When my firstborn, Stephen, was put into my arms, only minutes old, the rest of my life faded into the background. In the same way that the ultrasound passes through the mother's skin, muscle, and tissue to focus only on the baby, I felt that everything else in my life was only a structure that held a place for my divine purpose: motherhood.

Along the way, I've met many women who embraced the

concept of "having it all." Some have told me of how they plotted out their futures from the time they graduated from high school. First education, then career, then marriage while continuing a career, and then, sometime later, when they feel "in a good place financially" to have a child, they plan to be a mother. The reality is that there is no "having it all." Our female bodies are designed to carry children not on our timelines, but on God's. The facts of our biology tell us what God's wisdom thinks is best for both mother and child. I can say, as a woman who had her first baby at twenty-three and became a mother to her last baby at forty-two, that it's easier to enjoy yourself as a mother when you are younger. You just have more energy. I'm a more knowledgeable mom now to my youngest, but my older children experienced me as more playful. There will never be "the perfect time" to raise children. Children change every idea of how you think your life should go. That is a blessing. There is no job in existence that takes more time, focus, commitment, and love. And, for me, there will never be any job that gives me more joy and a feeling of accomplishment. As an older mom, now, I know better than to let anyone convince me that there is anything out there that is worth missing the opportunity to be a mother.

I've always loved the feeling of having a newborn's tiny fingers wrapped around one of mine, because it's a moment in time that will quickly go by. Soon that tiny hand will be big enough to grip a bottle, then hold the side of the crib to stand up, then be traced around on a page, then throw a football, then hold a diploma, then wear a wedding ring, then hold my grandchild.

Awe

Reverence and wonder, deep respect for the source of life.

$\mathscr{D}$ESSERT IS ALWAYS SAFE

Making the most important part of Sunday dinner, soon after my kids and I moved to Las Vegas in 2008. With Brianna.

*S*omewhere over Ohio, I start to register the anticipation in my taste buds. Even if I've managed to doze off, I know I will wake up when the captain says, "We should be landing in about twenty minutes." Then I start to count forward. Thirty minutes until I get off the plane in Philly. Fifteen minutes to wait for my bags. Forty minutes in the car.

I'm heading to QVC land. The studio sits on acres of vibrant, tree-filled property in Pennsylvania. In the fall, the trees lining the streets along the way look like a mosaic of harvest colors. But I'm not really focused on that right now.

During the flight, I looked over my notes and the photos for each of the porcelain dolls that I'll be showing live on air within a few hours. These are dolls that I've designed; I've handpicked each detail right down to the lace edging on their anklets. But I'm not really focused on that right now.

On my iPhone are at least thirty-five business e-mails that downloaded following my five-hour flight from Las Vegas. Almost all of them need an answer before the day is over. But I'm not really focused on that right now, either.

Once I'm in the car on my way to the QVC studio, my mind and my mouth are focused only on one thing: a milk shake.

It's not just any old milk shake. About fifteen minutes from the QVC studio is a local convenience store where you can fill up your tank with gas and get a milk shake, too. The shakes come in a sealed plastic cup that you set on a self-help mixing machine. Just push your button of choice, thick or regular, and presto: dessert time. The only inconvenience is choosing vanilla, strawberry, or chocolate.

It's almost sad that I haven't made any effort to divert my thinking pattern from "I want a milk shake." But it's because I'm traveling. I know it's a behavior that was conditioned in my childhood. Whenever we traveled, on the road, we would get to eat dessert as a meal, sometimes even two or three desserts.

I'm a dessert-loving Osmond. All of my brothers are as well. My kids rarely skip dessert, and I would guess that every single niece and nephew would choose sweet over savory any day. It's a sugar-driven legacy passed down from my mother. Thanks a lot, Mom!

My mother always kept a stash of chocolate hidden around the house in various places. I would sometimes find her near a closet door, nibbling on a square of chocolate. She would look over at me and grin and say, "Just a little afternoon pick-me-up." Now, when I look back at her life, I know that it must have been her way to combat her fatigue. I understand completely, Mom.

A good snack, especially something sweet, was my mother's way of giving both comfort and reward to her children. A job well done got a cookie or two, and a tough day ended with some cake and almost always ice cream. It was the instant smile producer for all eight of my brothers and me. When my mother was a child, at the tail end of the depression, sweets were a luxury saved for special events. When I was a child, desserts and baked goods were much more available, easier to make or buy, and affordable for almost every American family. Now it seems in many households that it is the only food group.

My mother loved making homemade treats and would page through magazines and cut out recipes and catalogue them in countless notebooks, always wanting to try baking something new. Of course, great farm-raised vegetables and fruits and nutritious meals were always a part of our everyday life if we were at home. My mother could even make eating the healthy food into a fun experience. She would sample a new salad recipe, and whichever child took an immediate liking to it had the salad named after him, and it would be forever known by that title. When it was time to make dinner, she might say, "Let's have Merrill's salad tonight."

Even our garden had personalized rows. Wayne cherished his corn on the cob rows. I had raspberry plants that were known as mine, and Donny was fiercely protective of his sweet peas. We each had our own favorites when it came to fruits and vegetables, which is most likely proof that people's taste buds are as unique to them as their hair and eye colors. I think my mother understood that because of her own eating issues.

My father, on the other hand, thought that food was a gift, God's bounty of the earth, and should never go to waste but be appreciated. I have vivid taste bud memories of countless mornings as a little girl from when we first moved to California and we all had to suffer through the delight my father found in harvesting the huge grapefruit tree in our backyard. This tree produced grapefruit like it had been injected with a fertility drug. Even the smallest new twig held on to a nasty, sour, three-pound yellow grapefruit. Every morning, my father would present each of us with a huge, sixteen-ounce glass of fresh-squeezed juice. My father relished every sip, but it put the rest of us in pain; it was like swallowing liquid aluminum mixed with WD-40. My brothers and I even attempted to "downsize" the crop by lobbing countless grapefruits over our fence into our neighbor's yard. We almost got away with it until Mrs. Nickeleye (who had a really good eye) called our father and insisted that we come over and take our "gifts" back home. I think even my mother tried to give large baskets of grapefruits away to our other neighbors so that we could be spared the tumblers of juice every morning. When she couldn't get rid of them, she would stir a tablespoon (or two or three) of sugar into each of our glasses to make the juice more drinkable.

I don't think my mother meant to leave us each with an insatiable sweet tooth. She developed her own during our years and years of touring the world as a family of entertainers. Eating dessert first was frequently her only option.

My mother's love for people around the world still has an effect today. I often get fan mail from people who remember how "sweet" my mother was. She loved every culture we visited and appreciated the beauty of their music, crafts, arts, architecture, rituals, and holidays. And the people loved her back, bringing her the best-loved foods of their country. What might have been a culinary delight to the locals would get to my tenderhearted mother right in her sensitive stomach. She never wanted to be rude, but if it wasn't a food that she recognized from the first decades of her life, it was doubtful that she would be able to chew and swallow it. Her mother was the same way. Grandma Davis would get queasy just at the sound of other people chewing. I don't remember her ever sitting at a table when my brothers were eating dinner. She would stand at the kitchen counter to eat, and then it was always a one-flavor food like a baked potato, some warm custard, or her favorite, vanilla ice cream, and she would keep Pepsi on hand to settle her stomach at a moment's notice. My mother was never introduced to foods with any kind of spice until she met my father.

Right after "One Bad Apple" became a number one hit for my brothers, we went on an extensive world tour. In my mother's journal from that spring and summer, she noted many times her inability to eat what was available. In Mexico City, one entry in May of 1975 read: *"Between shows, George* [my dad] *sent out for chicken. It still had feathers on it and was greasy. The boys and George were cleaning the dressing room when it arrived. When he saw the feathers on the chicken he just deposited it all into the garbage can. It was so funny."* My mother then had to lie on a couch until her feelings of nausea passed. Four days into our concert tour of Mexico, she wrote: *"I have only had onion soup and nuts since I've been here. I'm afraid to eat."* She probably thought she would fare better in Brussels the next week, only to find that she couldn't swallow the backstage meal that had been prepared to welcome us. She wrote, "*The sandwiches they served were raw hamburger and raw fish. Ugh! The cheese and the chocolate were good, though.*"

When our family was invited to dinner at the Malacca Palace in Malaysia and chilled monkey brains, a local delicacy, were part of the appetizer plate, my mother could barely sit at the table. In that case, she wasn't alone. We were all particularly chatty that day, so we had an excuse not to eat. After all, it's universal etiquette not to speak with your mouth full, isn't it?

My parents had no idea what we would be facing on the next leg of our tour, which was to London. Thousands of teenagers had filled the terminal at Heathrow Airport and were packed tightly against one another in the tiered outdoor balconies to see our family step off the airplane. They were stomping their feet, pounding their fists on the railings, and chanting, "We want the Osmonds. We want the Osmonds." Even more were waiting outside the airport terminal. This was before the days of high security. As we were being hustled off the plane, down the stairway, and to the limos that were waiting for us next to the plane, my brothers and I looked around awestruck. The noise of chanting was resounding off the walls—the voices of thousands of girls, some of them screaming and crying. My brothers got into the limos first, and I followed close behind. For some reason, I turned at the last moment and saw one of the balconies starting to sway and bend. Pieces of concrete were falling and people started to scream, but this was a different scream from before. The girls on the balcony below began to panic, fearing that they would be crushed. I was terrified for the girls, but the police were directing the limos to move on as quickly as possible. We read later that six girls had been injured, but not critically. After this, airport officials banned the Osmonds from flying in and out of Heathrow. They could no longer risk the possibility of people being critically injured and, at that time, didn't have the resources for crowd control.

We arrived at our hotel to find that it, too, was already mobbed by thousands of fans. They were trying to sneak in the service loading docks and climb up fire escape ladders. I think we were only there one night before the hotel manager told us that for our safety and the safety of his other hotel guests we would have to move on.

Our tour manager secretly found a flat, which belonged to a sheik, that we could rent and use as our home away from home. We thought that would solve the problem, only to find out that Osmond fans had posted themselves on almost every corner of that section of London. When they saw us on the move, they were able to decipher exactly which way the car had turned and discover our final destination. Smart kids, right? They managed this all before the days of cell phones or even pagers. We barely got into the flat before screaming fans surrounded it, day and night. I'm pretty certain the poor neighbors were never fans of ours after that short stay.

Finally, in an act of desperation, our tour manager moved us to a small castle in the countryside where the Jackson 5 had stayed a couple of months earlier and had managed to go undiscovered by the fans. And boy, was it ever undiscoverable. There wasn't a store within miles, which seemed like a nightmare to me at the time. I loved London culture and fashion, and there I was, stuck with heavy brocade drapery and candle-holding wall sconces. I felt as if I had been banished to the 1800s. There was no Disney princess charm to this castle for a young girl.

The promoter offered to hire a private cook for the castle, and my father thought that was a great idea, especially for the sake of my mother. He could tell that my mother had reached her limit of fish and chips, since she wouldn't even eat the fish. Even though my dad and I were adventurous eaters, trying everything that was offered at least once, he could see that my mother was suffering. My brothers, as children, were all "safe" eaters as well. They liked traditional cooking, and the only tradition they knew was American family style.

Our first day with the new cook on board, it appeared that my mother was finally going to be able to enjoy her first full meal since leaving California. After an afternoon of interviewing for the BBC, we arrived back at the castle to an amazing aroma. All of our faces lit up at the smell that we recognized as pot roast. We hurried to chairs around the dinner table as the food arrived on our plates. My mother smiled up at the cook and took a forkful to her mouth.

"This smelled so good when we came through the front door," my dad said. "What is it?"

We all waited for the answer because it didn't quite look like any pot roast we had ever eaten before.

The cook beamed and said, "I thought you'd like it. It's my specialty: kidney pie with oxtail."

My mother never wanted to be the center of attention, but she was that evening. All ten of us turned simultaneously to look at her. The forkful of kidney pie was already in her mouth, but her jaw wasn't moving. We all watched as a line of perspiration broke out along her upper lip, her skin took on a pale green tint, and she raised her hand to cover her mouth. She excused herself to the powder room and didn't return for about ten minutes. I believe my father and I braved our way through three or four of my brothers' plates so as not to offend the cook, but I definitely recall that my brothers and Mom each had two large helpings of the bread pudding the cook made for dessert. That may have been where it all started. Dessert was always safe.

That same night, Jimmy, who was eight years old, decided it would be hysterical to dress up as Dracula and jump out of a shadowy nook to scare the family. With his face powdered white, his eyebrows arched with black liner, and red lipstick covering his mouth, he leapt toward my poor recovering mother as she made her way to her bedroom. He flapped his black cape and yelled, "I vant to drrrink your blooooooddddd. Bwawhhhhhaaaahahahaha." My mother screamed, even though she knew right away that it was Jimmy. It probably seemed totally possible that a pint of O positive blood could very well be the standard after-dinner drink following a plate of kidney pie.

I don't even need to tell you what happened with the haggis in Scotland, do I? Yes, the very sight of tender morsels of sheep's liver and lungs boiled in the casing of some other organ was enough to give my mother and brothers PDSD (Predinner Stomach Disorder).

Touring the Asian countries was even more of a challenge to my mother's delicate sense of what was edible. On the streets, she would shield her eyes from the baskets of sun-dried toads, dehydrated pork ears, squid dangling from hooks, and small mammals that looked like they had been caught in a flash fire with their teeth still in place. When we went out to explore the fabric stores or local shops, she would do her best to avoid any type of food market.

For the most part, when it came to eating dinner, my mother would stay in the hotel and hope that something on the menu would be recognizably American. At one point in Japan, my mother was starving for a good meal. We asked Yoshi, the tour promoter, where we could find something that my mother would like to eat. Yoshi told us he knew the perfect restaurant, and we all set out to get my mother a feast that she could enjoy. Once we were seated, Yoshi pointed to a plastic food replica display dish that looked like stir-fried chicken. He smiled from ear to ear.

"This has no seafood. It's everybody's favorite," he told her.

My mother nodded her approval, and Yoshi ordered for her. The presentation of the food was beautiful, and the surroundings were peaceful. My mother seemed to really enjoy the food. My father was happy to see her finally be able to eat.

Halfway through, Yoshi asked my mother, "Do you like it?"

"Oh, yes," she said. "It's delicious. Thank you."

Yoshi smiled again. "Good," he said. "It's vegetables and fried white mouse."

My father tried to convince my mother that Yoshi was just pulling her leg, but even the mention of eating a rodent was all she could handle. She couldn't take even one more bite. This time she turned glow-in-the-dark green. She pushed back from the table and weaved through the restaurant quickly, a napkin covering her mouth. That evening was the end of my mother's willingness to experience any more Japanese restaurants.

After my father got her back to our hotel and found her a ginger ale to sip, he went out and bought some Japanese cookies and candy bars and whatever baked fruit pastries he could find, which is what my mother survived on for the next two weeks. Desserts were always safe.

My father and I would go off hand in hand on daddy-daughter excursions to sample the local cuisine, which could be anything from shark fin soup to pigeon eggs to sparrow spit stew. He always told me he was glad he had one "man" in the family. My mother rarely forced any of her children to eat what she couldn't. Since she found almost everything foreign to be unpalatable, unless it was recognizably chicken or beef, we kids took full advantage of her tender stomach. While we were on tour, and only then, we sometimes got to choose from the dessert menu for breakfast, lunch, and dinner.

Our family developed such a notable reputation for enjoying sweets that to this day, when Japanese fans come to Las Vegas to see the *Donny & Marie Show*, they bring us bags and bags of yummy Japanese candy.

My father never teased my mother about her sensitive stomach, and I never really understood why until I was an adolescent and my older brothers started to raise families of their own. My father was a cowboy and a true rancher at heart. He could brand cattle, break a horse, catch, scale, and gut a fish, milk a cow, and pluck a dead turkey without blinking. That was the way of life on a ranch, and my dad was fearless about all of it. However, there was one thing he absolutely could not stomach. Even though he was the father of nine children, my dad could not stand to change a dirty diaper. He would become completely nauseated and would feel like he was going to faint.

I remember one day on our ranch hearing my father call out, "Good morning," to me as I came outside after breakfast. I turned to see him wearing a long rubber glove up to his armpit, as he and the other ranch hands checked to see if the cattle were impregnated. I remember thinking to myself, "You can do that to a cow and you can't change a diaper? I'm not buying it, Dad! You just don't want to help with the diaper duty."

But it was no joke. One afternoon, my parents were at my brother Alan's home to babysit for the day. There were four little boys at that time, and the youngest was just learning to walk. My mother decided to go into town to the post office. My father got a concerned look on his face and said, "Don't be long, in case something happens."

Shortly after she left, the baby filled his diaper, and my father panicked. This was before people carried cell phones, so he knew that he was on his own. He let the baby wear it around for about an hour, hoping my mother would return quickly to clean up the situation. Once the baby started crying in discomfort, my father felt so bad for him, he knew he would have to take action. He called the other three boys into the house and herded them all into the bathroom, where he could keep an eye on them. His plan was to set the baby in the bathtub, remove the diaper and hose him down with the shower sprayer, so he wouldn't have to really look at or touch anything. As my mother told me the story, she arrived home and heard the shower running. Curious as to where the children were, she peeked into the bathroom to find my father and the older boys all crowded around the tub, in which the baby was standing. Dad pulled the tapes of the disposable diaper, and as soon as it came loose, he "tossed his cookies" all over the baby while the other three little boys looked on wide-eyed in shock and horror.

My mother said she exclaimed: "Oh good laws, George! What a mess." She moved my father to the side and grabbed the baby in a towel. My dad lay on the bathroom floor, sweaty, green, and trying to recover. Each of Alan's sons, with the exception of the poor baby, still remembers that incident. Who wouldn't? Post-Diaper Stress Disorder! Many grandkids remember going fishing or building a birdhouse with their grandpa; those three boys remember the day Grandpa threw up on their little brother.

This just proved to me that all people have an issue with at least one thing that they can't stomach. Even my steady army sergeant–rancher father, who had toured the world and could eat almost any type of food, could be taken down by a full diaper! All of my brothers inherited my mother's tender stomach and her sweet tooth, but thankfully for their wives' sake, none of them inherited my father's inability to change a diaper.

While pregnant with my third child, I had a horrible bout of morning sickness that involved a carryout pizza; to this day, the smell of hot pizza resting in a cardboard box can make my mouth water . . . but not in a good way. I still have to be in a very specific frame of mind to enjoy pizza.

Like my mother, I can be guilty of making sugar a major food group when I travel. It's one of the reasons I'm a Nutrisystem girl. You can have for lunch a Fudge Graham bar, which tastes like a delicious dessert, and be nutritionally set! After all, I can't always risk what might be hidden in the sauce at certain restaurants or wondering how long the chicken was left out on the counter. And I admit that—like mother, like daughter—I've given in a few times when my kids wrinkled their noses at what was on offer when we went out on tour together. I have encouraged my kids to be more adventurous in their dining selections, like their grandpa. They have all liked sushi since they were small. But still, my most daring eater will sometimes get a little green at the thought of dinner looking back at him. While we have been touring internationally, there have been days when we've had cookies for breakfast, doughnuts for lunch, and milk shakes for dinner. I'm not proud of it. But at least I'm not up all night with a kid or two with travel-related food poisoning!

Of course, the sugar-as-main-course meals stop when the tour ends, and balanced meals are routine again.

All of my kids have gone through phases of not liking vegetables, even if I prepare them. When I'd encourage them to eat a salad, my sons used to drown one sliver of cucumber in a cup of ranch dressing. I've seen my kids hide green beans under the edge of their plates or fill their mouths and then pretend to sneeze into napkins and throw them away. After eight children, I'm onto all of their tricks. Some of my kids will claim that they "ate a spinach salad" when all that really happened is the bacon bits and hard-boiled eggs got grazed off the top of it.

Even though I know the secrets of their disappearing tricks, I choose not to get into a power struggle with my kids, insisting that every vegetable be eaten. I have been invited to family dinners at the homes of friends and watched a dinner conversation be ruined by an upset child being forced to eat.

I've also known children who grew up with very restrictive parents who insisted on low-fat, no-sugar, and even no-dairy diets. I've noticed an interesting backlash, in that as soon as the kids have more independence, they tend to overindulge in everything that was restricted early in life. I also have to wonder if there is a correlation between our current culture and our pursuit of "healthy" eating, wherein we count every calorie and study every ingredient, and the rise in eating disorders such as bulimia and anorexia among children. My mother's motto when it came to our eating habits was "Everything in moderation."

For the most part, I don't overly stress about what my kids eat, especially since I don't keep many unhealthy snack foods in the house. I found that if healthier food is just what's around, instead of insisted upon, it's usually tried and usually liked.

Sugar snap peas, butternut squash, fresh chopped salsa, and edamame in the pods have produced a willing smile on all of their faces, though I'm careful to make sure they don't see me noticing that they like them. Saturday, though, is the morning that my kids know they can have a big bowl of their favorite sugary cereal. School mornings it's always oatmeal or eggs or a whole-grain cereal.

When Donny and I were young, we called broccoli "poisoned trees." We dreaded eating it and made sure our mother noticed the severity of our dislike if she served it for any meal. We would sit at the table and chew the broccoli spears slowly, with exaggerated grimaces on our faces. Then we would pretend to choke and fall unconscious. I'm sure our mother found it all very amusing. While our older brothers could entertain any dinner guests by singing four-part harmony, I knew I could probably bring the curtain down with my dramatic paraphrasing of Shakespeare's Juliet in her dying speech: "What's here? Poison broccoli trees, I see, hath been his timeless end." Our one saving grace was that it didn't grow in the garden, so we didn't have to suffer through it too often.

For my own kids, I did discover one clever way to prepare broccoli without even a whine being heard. Put your cooked broccoli into the blender and then mix it into the mashed potatoes! Most children will eat mashed potatoes. In the same way I did as a child, my kids find that a pale shade of green can be unusually funny.

Since I have to be away from home five nights a week to do our show at the Flamingo, I really cherish the times we can have family dinners. If the older kids and my daughter-in-law, Claire, are in town and can join us, it's the best night ever for me as a mother. I want us to all enjoy one another's company as a family group and not have to focus on the food groups.

I appreciate that my mother knew, because of her own sensitive taste buds, that food tastes are very individual, but they can also change as a person gets older. I think if my mother had forced asparagus on me as a child, I never would have tried it again as an adult and fallen in love with the way it tastes. And in a real twist, I now prefer fresh-squeezed grapefruit juice to any sugary drink! However, there are going to be the special occasion days when junk food rules the plate and the palate, and that's okay once in a while.

My brother Jimmy and his wife and four children stayed at my home the night before my wedding in 2011. My kids love having their cousins around to play with, so they stay up late and have extra treats. For breakfast the next morning, I put out fresh fruit plates, eggs, and whole wheat toast. When I walked into the kitchen, I found eight kids gathered around the table, all eating bowls of sugary cereal in various shapes and neon colors. Jimmy hovered nearby, enjoying his own bowl, wearing a grin. He just shrugged. "Your pantry was too healthy. I had to make a grocery store run. What can I say? I'm my mother's son." When I told the kids they should have some fruit with their cereal, my eleven-year-old replied, "This is fruit-flavored cereal." The truth is, if I hadn't had to squeeze into my original wedding dress from 1982 in the next three hours, I would have happily joined them.

At QVC, I'll often do three shows in one day, with product design or other business meetings in between. By the time we are heading back to the airport, I'm pretty tired because I may have been talking for almost eight hours straight. It can wear on the vocal cords. So I always stop to get something soothing for my rough, dry throat. What's more soothing than a cold milk shake or two? Shhhh. Please don't tell my kids.

Endurance

The power to bear an unpleasant or difficult process or situation without giving way. Practicing patience when obstacles arise.

MARIE OSMOND

My daughters Rachael, Brianna and Abigail, 2012. Yes, they all inherited my sugar cravings. Brianna made killer cupcakes!

MALLARD

My Mallard at age one, Michael Bryan, forever imprinted on my heart and soul.

This week there will be another wave. I can feel the tug on me. I know I'll be pulled under for a while, but now I can recover a little bit faster, catch my breath, and get back on my feet. Never easier, only sooner.

I'm writing this two years to the day after my son Michael left this earth at age eighteen. I have had countless waves of knockdown grief in these past two years. The respites of peace have become a little longer; but then, like the ocean, the bottomless sorrow I feel from losing my son stirs, builds, and then crashes over me once more. My family understands and my friends stay close by, but no one can make it better. After the first twenty-four hours of feeling the kind of grief that turns you inside out when you find out that your child has died, you realize that no one can ever make it better. Every day, even now, I stand in the shallows of an underlying sadness, fully aware that, at any time, another wave will pull me into the depths of anguish. It's an inconceivable sorority of sisters that I have been initiated into without a choice: women who have lost a child. Only through my faith in God do I have the courage to get back onto my feet.

Four nights a week, right after our Las Vegas show, Donny and I do a "Meet 'n Greet" where we chat with people who have bought a VIP seat for that evening's performance. We are one of the few shows on the Strip to offer one. I love to meet and talk with the audience members. One night, about six months before Michael died, I noticed a woman standing off to the side who didn't have a "Meet 'n Greet" pass. Her expression was emotionless and hollow. She happened to be an acquaintance of my executive assistant, but they had lost touch many years ago. Without knowing why, I had a strong feeling that I should talk to her. I had seen the look in her eyes before: the look of not really being engaged in life, but merely existing in it. I had witnessed that look in my own mirror, when I experienced postpartum depression. I told my assistant to ask the woman to wait, even though I couldn't really believe I was inviting this relative stranger to my dressing room. On most evenings, after the show and the "Meet 'n Greet," I hurry to get out of my costume and home to my kids and my husband. But on this night, I knew I had to follow my intuition and hear what this woman had to say.

There was very little small talk between us right from the start. She told me that she could no longer live with her grief over losing her teenage son two months before. She had come to Las Vegas, by herself, to end her life far from where her family members would be the first to find her. She had planned to go straight to her room once she checked in, but something made her feel like she should get a ticket to see our show. She thought it would be something to take her mind off of what she was about to do. After the show she had been drawn to this side room where we were holding the "Meet 'n Greet." Once there, she saw my executive assistant, a friend she hadn't seen in two decades. This hadn't been in her plans.

Her son was seventeen years old and he had been out with friends at a party. The woman told me that although she never suspected her son had any drug problems, he had been found at this party dead of a massive overdose. The coroner had told her that the high level of drugs in his system had caused cardiac arrest. The look on her face now seemed to mirror the resigned anguish she felt inside. She had tortured herself endlessly, asking, "Why did this happen?" and "how" could she have saved him? Since there would never be a clear answer to either question, she had decided not to save herself, either. She had managed to gather enough prescription medication to go to sleep and not wake up. She had her room key and her bottles of pills. She was ready.

I somehow knew that I needed to keep listening to this woman, at least until she felt heard and understood. I thought that I could empathize with her pain. As one of the founders of Children's Miracle Network, I'd been with quite a few women who have lost a child to illness or accident. But you don't have to experience it to comprehend the anguish. Any mother can imagine what it would feel like to lose a child. Most of us probably had the same thought as we held our brand-new babies for the first time: "I love this child so much, I will protect her or him from any harm, even with my own life."

As the night went on, I found myself in a silent plea to God to help me know what to say to this woman, who was suffering so deeply. To my shock, it came into my heart to say something I would never say to a stranger: "Even if your son had survived the cardiac arrest and the overdose, he would never have been like your son again. His brain damage would have been very severe. Your son is free of a lifelong struggle that might have been much more painful for both of you."

As soon as the words were out, I almost apologized for saying them. How could I possibly know if that was true? I only knew that I had to be the one to say it to her.

The woman became calmer as we talked and by the end of the evening, she promised me that she would go home and seek grief counseling. I gave her my e-mail address and asked her to keep me posted, and I had a late-night dinner sent to her room to make sure she knew I was supporting her decision to stay strong and go home to her family.

About two weeks later, she e-mailed me to say that the full autopsy report had come back with the very conclusion I had told that evening without knowing why. The same drugs that caused his heart to stop working had quickly damaged her son's brain beyond recovery. She wrote that I was a "mercy from a loving God." Little did I know then the extent of "mercy" I would need from a loving God only a few months into my future. She then wrote, "I know you were inspired that night because not only did your words cause me to think with more clarity, but on the way home I found a book someone had left behind in the airplane seat pocket. It was the exact book you had recommended. It was very helpful."

The very next night during the "Meet 'n Greet," another woman gave me a hug and said, "Oh, Marie. You've been through depression, abuse, divorce, kids in rehab, the death of your parents, illness, and challenges. What haven't you been through?" Thinking about the grieving mother the night before, I answered, "I haven't lost a child. That would be the worst thing that could happen."

On February 26, 2010, the "worst thing that could happen" happened. My sweet son left me, his sisters and brothers, family and friends, by jumping from the balcony of his eighth-floor college apartment in downtown Los Angeles. Even as I write this, two full years later, I want to cry out, "Please, don't let this be true." What I wouldn't give to wrap my arms around my child one more time.

When Michael was about two years old, his older brother, Stephen, gave him the nickname "Mallard." All of my kids have had nicknames that they were called more than their actual names until they were about twelve years old, when the nicknames started to embarrass them in public. Jessica's was "Angelic," usually shortened to "Gelic," Rachael's was "Sweetness," and Brandon's was "Smiley," for being the happiest baby of all. Brianna was "Princess," because from birth she had a royal attitude, but sometimes "Piranha," because, even though she was my most girly girl, she was inclined to chomping down on people as a toddler. Matthew had to suffer through "Bubbie" and then "Bubbalicious," most often shortened to "Lish."

Michael was the one who gave Abigail her nickname of "Baster," and his reasons were always a mystery, but it had something to do with a turkey. The kids were all in the kitchen on Thanksgiving morning, and Michael pulled the baster out of the drawer, tapped Abigail once on each shoulder, and said, "Thy nickname shall be Baster. So it is written. So shall it be done." I guess it had something to do with a baster's function, she being a "little squirt" at that time.

Michael's nickname, "Mallard," had to do with the shape of his adorable top lip. When you looked at his face in profile, his thin little upper lip had a slight curl to it and overlapped his lower lip a tiny bit, giving him the appearance of a baby duck. This changed, by age seven, to look completely normal as his face grew, but the nickname stuck.

I never realized how fully his nickname actually fit his personality until Abigail wanted to see a photograph of a mallard to see if it really did look like Mike, and together we read a teacher's helper page of fun facts on the Internet.

The Mallard duck is one of the most adaptable birds in the world and can be found in North America, Europe, and Asia.

Michael was definitely an adaptable and adventuresome child, especially when it came to touring with me both nationally and internationally. Even though he was small for his age until about fifteen, and very reserved around new people, he was usually the first one in the car, on the plane, or on the bus ready for an adventure. One time, when he was about five, Michael jumped in a taxicab in Hong Kong without the driver knowing it. The cab started to pull away with all of us chasing down the street waving our arms. I was always having to tell him to wait for me. He was also an avid observer, checking out every new social situation, which reminded me of myself as a small child. I would stand on the sidelines and watch for a while because I wanted to think things over and connect the dots before I jumped into a situation with people I didn't know. Michael was the same way.

Michael was intrigued by every new place we visited, anywhere in the world. He absorbed the flavors of the culture, especially the art, designs, and style of the region. Sometimes, he adapted to it all a bit too much. In 1998, after I completed my run on Broadway as Anna in *The King and I*, I was invited to play Maria in *The Sound of Music* on a prestigious tour through Southeast Asia. I knew that it was a "once-in-a-lifetime" opportunity and that it would be a unique experience for my children. Well, the temperatures that summer were blazing hot, and my fourteen-year-old, Stephen, began to envy the clean-shaven heads of the Buddhist monks he would see on the streets. Halfway through the tour, he begged me to let him have his hair shaved off.

My hairdresser on the tour said she would give him his new look. The rest of the family stood by and watched as Stephen's full head of hair fell to the floor, and the remaining stubble was taken off with shaving cream and a razor. At one point the razor nicked his scalp and a small trickle of blood went around his ear, but he was happy with his new look.

After we had all piled back in to our touring van and were driving off, Michael ran his hands through his own curly dark blond hair and started to cry. I thought he might be upset that Stephen had shaved his head, and so I told him, "It's okay. You can keep your hair." I had it wrong. As a small child, Michael had had a hard time pronouncing the letter "l," so it was pretty tough to keep a straight face when he looked up at me and sobbed, "I want to be bawed and bweeding wike Stephen." What could I say? He wanted to be a part of the trend. Fifteen minutes later, I had a bald five-year-old grinning ear to ear next to his older brother. Then I looked over at Jessica, who was about nine at the time and who always loved wearing her hair short. "Don't even think about it," I said.

Like many boys, Michael never fully appreciated his gorgeous curly hair, and after age fourteen, he always kept his hair less than a half inch long to make sure he didn't have to deal with the curl. I remember when we first moved to Las Vegas, Michael was in the bathroom with his electric clippers, getting ready for his first day as a senior in high school, and ten-year-old Brandon decided that he wanted to be "bald and bleeding," too. Mike granted his wish, much to my dismay, shaving off Brandon's straight blond locks; within two minutes, he looked like he was heading to boot camp instead of fifth grade. After the initial daring wore off, being bald didn't seem like such a great idea and Brandon took to wearing a hat every day until his hair grew out a bit. Unfortunately, wearing a wool beanie in Las Vegas when it's 105 degrees isn't all that fun.

Mallards often have a comic nature.

It was impossible for anyone in the family to stay upset or angry if Michael was around. No matter what the grievance was, Mike would have the whole room laughing in a matter of minutes. He would come up with hysterical voices, just off the cuff, and characters who had a series of facial expressions that no one else could pull off. One, in particular, was called simply "the Face" and involved scrunching up his face to resemble a pouting shar-pei dog, with about seventeen folds of skin from his hairline to his chin. Michael, with his sensitive heart, couldn't stand to be around people who argued or hurt someone else's feelings on purpose, so he would defuse any negative situation with laughter. He could keep anyone entertained, from an eight-month-old to his eighty-nine-year-old grandfather.

Even as a very little boy, Mike would take notice of and reach out to those who were marginalized because they were different, and figure out a way to make them smile. One afternoon when he was a preschooler, we made a quick stop at McDonald's for a late lunch. Near the front door, sitting on the curb, was a man who was obviously homeless. Michael stopped in his tracks and wouldn't go in the restaurant. He tugged on my arm impatiently. "Mommy, wait. Buy him a hangaburger," which is what he called hamburgers as a little boy. Before he would even order anything for himself, Michael had to take a full bag of food to the man outside of the door.

During his elementary school years, he would volunteer to help any child with a handicap get through their day. His favorite extracurricular activity was volunteering in the special-education classes and coming up with projects for the kids like making cars out of Twinkies and stringing beaded friendship bracelets. He would come home and tell me stories of how he loved being with them and how he would make them laugh and smile. Michael was always drawn to the pureness of spirit and honest reactions in these special children. As he got older, he would never pass any person who appeared to be homeless without opening his wallet and giving what he could. If he only had a twenty-dollar bill, then he would give the homeless person the twenty dollars.

Even though he was almost always shorter and smaller than most of the boys in his age group, if anyone else talked disrespectfully to or about his sisters, he would stand up for their integrity. If there was someone who fit the quote "It's the quiet ones you've got to watch out for," it was Michael, but only when it came to someone picking on his family or friends. I know he took quite a few bullies by surprise. He never initiated any confrontations, but he didn't back down from a bully. They never messed with him or his sisters again.

When Mike was eleven, he wanted to play tackle football. It made me nervous because the other boys on the teams were about four inches taller and thirty pounds heavier than Michael. Parents in the bleachers would often point him out with a remark or two about how little he was. But as with everything else, Mike threw his whole heart into playing. As it turned out, being short and quick, with a lot of upper body strength, worked in his favor. He was tough to catch up to, could duck under long, clumsy arms, and managed to become one of the best players on the team both as a running back and a defensive lineman. Not only could Mike make anyone laugh, he could have the last laugh, too.

The Mallard duckling must be ready to survive on his own shortly after hatching.

I adopted Michael a few days after his birth. His birth mother was an unwed teenager whose pregnancy was unplanned, and tragically Mike's teenage birth dad was killed in a car accident before the baby was born. To protect his birth mother's privacy, I want only to relay one part of her story in connection with my son.

When Michael was thirteen years old, a woman rang our doorbell and identified herself as his birth mother. The facial features were so similar, it was obvious she was telling the truth. She brought photo albums of herself as a teenager and also of the boy who was Mike's birth father, and she had pictures from when she was pregnant and one of the day Mike was born. She told us that she didn't want to intrude on his life and wanted only to see him and know he was okay. We were hesitant and wanted time to think it all through, but suddenly Michael and the older kids came up the stairs from the rec room, where they had been watching TV. I decided to introduce her to Michael, who could already tell who she was because of their similarities. They had the exact same chin and eyes. We all sat down and talked for over an hour, with her telling Michael the story of her pregnancy and his birth. Before she left, she gave us an address and phone number to reach her, if we wanted. Michael was intrigued and excited at meeting her, and I sensed that, as he hugged her good-bye, a part of his sensitive teenage heart must have been feeling that the missing piece of his history had been restored.

About a week later, Mike tentatively asked if he could send her flowers. It was Mother's Day, and he was very hesitant to ask me, thinking it would hurt my feelings. I told him that I thought it was a nice idea. We picked out a gorgeous bouquet online and had them delivered to her at the address she had given us. This is where the "happy ending" that many adoptive children probably hope for ran into reality. The flowers were returned as undeliverable. When Mike tried to call, the number had been disconnected. She had already moved on to a new location, and there was no forwarding address. She didn't stay in his life as he had hoped she would. Sometime later she sent him a card with an address and phone number, and he felt hopeful again. For the most part, though, she left his calls and letters unanswered, only responding every so often.

Years later, she told me that her intention was to let us have our life with our son and that she didn't want to intrude. She also admitted that she had suffered a lifelong struggle with depression and some addictions, but at that time, we were left to puzzle this out on our own. I wouldn't want her to feel any accusations coming from me about her struggles. I didn't hold a judgment about it when I found out, and I certainly don't now. I always admire that, as a teenager, she was able to set her own needs aside and, realizing that she didn't have the experience or resources to raise her child, give him the best opportunity to have a good life. I know she never intended to disappoint my son, ever. I think her hard life and struggle with severe depression made it almost impossible for her to know what the next day would hold. I have a deep empathy for her burden. She's a beautiful spirit who has been down a very tough and similar path, having been mostly alone and also adopted as an infant.

When Michael passed away, I had a family member locate her to let her know. Then, at my invitation, she came to his memorial service. She was completely heartbroken, and she and I cried throughout the service and at the grave site. As I told her that day, she had given me the best gift ever, my son.

When Michael first met his birth mother, I hoped that the association would be positive for him, but it seemed to confuse him at an age when he needed the most stability. I have rethought my actions many, many times. Perhaps we should have used more caution in letting her come into the house that first day or made sure that Michael didn't meet her until he was older and could understand her life story. I've always wanted to be straightforward with my children about their adoptions, and I've never felt that it was my right to withhold any information that I had about their birth parents when they asked about them. I still try to look at it all through my children's eyes; I know that I would be curious and want to know about my birth parents, too.

Michael started asking me about his birth mother when he was about seven years old. It was a time of big changes in our lives.

Shortly after his seventh birthday, I had to relocate the whole family to the Los Angeles area to tape the *Donny & Marie* talk show five days a week. After being the baby in the family for four and a half years, Mike also had to adjust to having two new siblings, Brandon and Brianna, join the family less than one year apart. My career hours shifted from working every evening in a Broadway show to being out of the house and on my way to the studio, usually from before the kids went to school until almost dinnertime. At the studio, I had a nursery/playroom set up next to my dressing room so I could have my babysitter bring the preschoolers, once they were awake and dressed, to be with me almost every day, but Michael had to be in school. The three older kids seemed to be at ages where they were more independent, which in a way was also not great for Mike. They had rigorous after-school schedules that included music lessons, karate, dance classes, sports, and other activities. Michael was often a passenger in this kid taxi service. As often as possible, the babysitter would drive Mike and the older kids to the studio to be with me, but being at a TV studio loses its charm for a kid pretty quickly, especially when there are no other kids around, and being quiet in a TV studio is almost always the order of the moment.

I resigned myself to the fact that this is how I made my living. I was grateful that I had this opportunity and all the benefits it provided, like the chance to have my babies with me at work. Even though I was away from the older kids all day, I thought that they were all getting sufficient attention, since they had a full-time babysitter and their father with them at home.

I've read books and articles by quite a few child experts who seem to agree that ages seven and eight are years of major developmental changes for a child, most having to do with the shape and the biology of the brain. It's the time when children gain much more reasoning power; they start to figure out how their actions produce cause and effect, the difference between right and wrong, and how they fit into the big picture of family and community. It's the age when kids start to worry less about dangers that are imagined, like monsters and ghosts, and more about real issues, like not being popular with their peers because they are different. They also identify with the value system their parents hold and start to apply it to their own lives. Not only was Michael probably trying to figure out the male-role-model aspect—we also went through another big life-altering change: In 1998, at age thirty-nine, three months into the first season of the *Donny & Marie* talk show, I found myself unexpectedly pregnant.

Getting pregnant had always been a challenge for me, which is one of the reasons I knew, early on, that some of my children would not come through me, but would still be my children. I always say, "Some of my children are adopted, but I can't remember which ones." People usually smile at that statement but it really is true for me. There is no differentiation in my feelings about any of my children. I felt total, unconditional love for each child the moment he or she was placed in my arms. Every one of my children will tell you that there is no difference between them. They are brothers and sisters, and being adopted or not has rarely been a topic of conversation among them. When people have asked them about it, they seem to all shrug it off as if the answer to the question were something as obvious as "Four of us have brown eyes, two have blue, and two have hazel."

However, after I gave birth in 1999 I experienced the darkest personal time of my life with postpartum depression. I had gained an extra sixty-five pounds (yes, sixty-five!!), and my hormones were at a record low, which wasn't discovered until months later. (There was little information available about postpartum depression in those days.) My baby boy was born two weeks into a six-week hiatus from the *Donny & Marie* talk show, so I had exactly four weeks before season two began to get back into shape, fit into my prepregnancy wardrobe, update my look, and be ready to step back onto the talk show set, fresh, happy, funny, and ready to go. For the publicity shots, they took my picture in a black top over black pants and then later digitally removed the excess pounds from my waist, arms, hips, and even my face.

I was in a downward spiral but my doctor labeled it the

"baby blues." I told him that I had given birth before and remembered the baby blues. What I was feeling this time was three times more severe than baby blues. I was put on an antidepressant and a synthetic hormone that only exacerbated my problems. I felt I had no one to talk to about what I was going through because, in a self-loathing way, I thought I must have been overreacting. After all, having the baby blues was something millions of women went through for a week or two. Little did I know that I was among the 10 to 20 percent of women who suffer severe depression following childbirth—depression that often goes ignored. Before giving birth, I would have told you that I had it all together and could handle almost anything. I had my thirty-five-year career in show business, my six children, a thirteen-year marriage, a national charity, a successful line of porcelain dolls, various awards, hit songs, and a long résumé. I thought I was a pretty tough broad!! I had worked my whole life. I had experienced both the good and the bad, and I wasn't naive about any of it. I truly believed that it would take a lot to knock me off course. Little did I know that it wouldn't take much at all: only a seven-pound-eleven-ounce baby boy. I named him "Matthew," which means "God's gift." And, truly, in the big picture, his birth brought a change and an understanding to my life that has been a gift. But at that time, so much was unknown about postpartum depression that I was left "a hot mess," as my teenagers would have described it. I couldn't figure out why I couldn't get a grip on my emotions, and the shame I had about feeling miserable during what was supposed to be "the happiest time in a woman's life" made me want to hide away from the world. I wished I could "snap out of it," not realizing that the odds of "snapping out of it" were extremely stacked against me. Recently, I spoke to a pregnancy group, and I asked how many of the women knew the risk factors of postpartum depression. No one raised her hand. There are eighteen known risk factors, and as I discovered after months of misery, I had seventeen of them. When I wrote about all of this in my book *Behind the Smile*, I was the first celebrity to go "public," and I did it because I didn't want other women to struggle for as long as I did without answers or, at the very least, some direction for finding help.

On my darkest day with postpartum depression, I handed my infant to a babysitter who was there to help me, gave her a credit card and said, "Take care of my kids."

I got in my car and drove up the Pacific Coast Highway for about *nine* hours.

I had no idea where I was going or why; I only knew that I wasn't in any frame of mind to be of use to anyone, especially my own children. My heart was breaking into a million pieces, because I saw myself as a complete failure in all areas: as a mother, a wife, a businesswoman, and an entertainer. Even as a friend.

Every moment of depression feels like all of your thoughts and emotional reactions are the truth, the total reality, and it's a struggle to convince yourself otherwise. For me, it was as if my eyes had sunk into the back of my head and I was viewing life from a dim and distant perspective. It's hard to see the big picture or hope on the horizon because you feel so removed from life. Depression turns your thoughts inward, which also makes it a seemingly selfish disease. You are consumed by the problems you are going through when you are depressed. People who care about you may be all around you; but you don't see it that way. It feels like you are all alone. Normal thinking and reactions are altered to where everything seems like a reflection of your failure. Any little thing that isn't going right suddenly seems to be your fault or a result of your own worthlessness. You don't keep track of things well or even have the energy to invest in what you are trying to do anymore, down to the smallest task.

Because of the way I felt on that July evening—scared, desperate, wondering how I could come up with the energy to cope until tomorrow or to face going back to my family and work—I have an idea of the hopelessness that my son was feeling on that February night eleven years later. The difference is, my son in his eighteen years didn't yet have the life experience to know that he wouldn't always feel so bad. With age comes wisdom that pulls you through the worst times, knowing that you have been down before and somehow came back to see a glimmer of hope ahead. Even though I wished that I could lie down and never wake up again, it still registered with me, somewhere in my right brain, that I would eventually find the help I needed. I had thirty-nine years of life experience and could lean more on a mature faith that God had not abandoned me and that He would see me through somehow. Yet even with my faith, I was in desperate need of some reassurance that it would eventually be okay again.

It was a phone call from my mother that finally got through to me. When I couldn't drive another mile, I checked into some no-tell motel halfway up the coast of California. My room was on the ground floor, with a sliding glass door that was jammed closed and towels that felt like cardboard boxes. Even the toilet had a paper strip covering the seat that claimed it was "sanitized." I knew it probably wasn't the safest place to be, but I didn't really care, considering I was mostly concentrating on remembering to breathe in and out. When my mother finally reached me, she told me something I never knew about her: She had felt the same way following the birth of my younger brother, Jimmy. She had been exhausted and overweight and had to face the daily responsibility of nine children. She thought she would never feel joy again. As I lay exhausted on top of the faded bedspread, she told me that one day she handed Jimmy to my father and told him that she had to leave for a while. In a bleary state of deep postpartum depression, not that she had ever heard the term, my mother got in the car and drove up the coast of California the same way I had done!

Through my mother's story, I felt comforted, and then I felt an increasing sense of hope. Over time, I started to accept my own experience. I knew that if my mother could overcome her depression, then I would be able to, as well.

It may be that the greatest gift you can give to a severely depressed person is your own story of battling depression so that they don't feel so alone. When I later asked my mother why she had never told me about her experience with postpartum depression, she admitted that she was ashamed of her feelings and thought she was being weak. It's terrible that the misconception remains widespread today. Depression is a real disease, not a sign that someone is wallowing in self-pity. Think about it: What person would ever choose to feel that bad? Shaming or scolding a depressed person only adds fuel to their feelings of not ever being good enough or able to cope.

Mallard ducks feed both day and night.

When Abigail and I read this next fun fact about mallards, we both laughed. There was no question about that similarity. My son was always up for a good meal. Along with absorbing all the sights and sounds of every culture, Mike loved to eat. In more than half of the photos that I have of Mike as a child, he is grinning over some type of culinary treat. At age eight, when most kids want a Chuck E. Cheese birthday party, Mike chose a sushi buffet. The other parents at the party loved it, but the classmates he invited waited to eat until the cake rolled out. Mike consumed his share of microwavable pizza bagels during his childhood, too, but if there was an option for something more ethnic with more distinctive flavors, he would almost always make that choice. The summer before he started college, the family spent a week in Mazatlán, Mexico. Mike wanted to try every local taco and burrito stand, and the hotter the salsa and jalapeños, the better. Even the locals were impressed with Mike's ability to heap on the heat.

A few months after Michael passed away, I took the kids to

Mazatlán again, during their spring break, just to be together as a family. After a day of long talks and walks on the beach, we went to get burritos at Mike's favorite restaurant. Brandon asked, "Which salsa would Mike get for his burrito?" I tried to warn him that it would be spicy, but Brandon poured it on in tribute to his older brother. About five minutes later, my blond-haired, blue-eyed boy was more like red, white, and blue!

In the same way that Mike loved all the culinary variety offered in this world, he also had a growing appetite for music. He listened to all types of music, including classical, world, jazz, reggae, and rap. He appreciated the true pioneers of any musical form and seemed to understand the composition of music much more naturally than most teenage boys. He could tell you what was great about both Frank Sinatra and Joss Stone. He loved Joni Mitchell and Bob Marley, but also wanted to listen to Mötley Crüe.

I could always tell when Michael was the last person in the car, because as soon as I would turn the key in the ignition some form of classic rock, like Jimi Hendrix or the Doors, would pound out of the dashboard speakers. My father, who also loved all types of music and instruments, decided to learn to play the ukulele at age eighty-nine, and Michael took up the same challenge for himself. Michael taught himself to play the ukulele, acoustic guitar, bass guitar, drums, and piano. He would compose orchestrated songs by recording each instrument separately and then mix his own music on his computer.

In my solo touring show, *A Little Bit Country . . . and a Whole Lot More*, I always sing "Over the Rainbow." As a child, I strongly identified with what I knew of Judy Garland as a young girl. She always seemed to look how I felt: alone in a crowd. From my earliest memories, my older brothers were already TV sensations on the *Andy Williams Show*, and they soon became a pop group whom young girls adored. Being the only female in this clan often left me feeling like an outsider. Plus, my brothers were so much prettier than me! They had thick, wavy hair; my hair was stick straight and stringy, with greasy bangs that matted to my forehead. They had eyelashes that went on for days; I guess God knew I could just buy mine and glue them on! There was something about the song "Over the Rainbow" that gave me hope and courage as a child of nine or ten. The lyrics "Why, oh, why can't I?" reminded me that if I applied myself, I could have a career as a singer, too. Michael also loved the song. Being the middle child, like my brother Merrill, who was the middle man in our family, I'm certain he often felt overlooked or like a small boat in a big sea of siblings. The best Mother's Day gift I've ever been given was presented to me on the last Mother's Day I was to celebrate with my son. Michael and Rachael learned "Over the Rainbow" on ukulele and guitar and played and sang it to me together. I wish I had videotaped that, but the memory is still with me, always.

Writing and playing music fed my son's creative soul in his early teenage years. It was a way for him to express himself creatively while staying out of the spotlight, as he preferred.

As a mother, I want my kids to experience the best that life and culture have to offer, which is why I try to limit what kinds of music my kids listen to and the video games they play. They don't like it; but I know too much now about the effect of negative music and violent games. I have a number of dear friends whose children became troubled, pessimistic, angry young adults who eventually turned to some form of mind-altering drugs or alcohol. In every case, the parents can point to a correlation between when their child started having emotional troubles and when they started listening to dark music or playing overly violent video games, filled with negative language or rage. Even the children who are now adults and in recovery have told me that the hours they spent listening to dark music went hand in hand with their subsequent problems.

One young man, the son of one of the engineers at the studio where I record, went through a number of rehab programs and would be okay for a couple of months and then give in to his addictions, eventually getting arrested and serving time in prison. Finally, he saw a therapist who told him that he had to completely avoid any music he listened to from the time he started having problems. The therapist explained that the music was emotionally transporting him back to a place of depression and addiction and that it could even create a biological reaction in his body, making it extremely difficult to resist a relapse. He has been able to stay drug-free since making the decision to follow this therapist's advice.

Michael's own issues with drug abuse coincided with listening to music with dark or violent lyrics: what he called "gangsta rap." I'm not talking about the poetic-type rap of artists like Will Smith, Usher, or Lauryn Hill; I'm referring to rap that glorifies thug behavior and that became very popular when Mike was starting high school, even where kids had no concept of an urban lifestyle. At the same time, he began attending parties in the homes of his friends. Most of them were innocent enough, but I should have looked deeper and asked more direct questions regarding the who, what, and where. I didn't want my teenagers to feel that I didn't trust them. Now I know better. Peer pressure can cause teenagers, especially sensitive or shy ones like my son, to go against what they know is "right" for the sake of being accepted into a group. I later discovered that some of these gatherings were what are called "pharm parties," to which kids brought whatever miscellaneous drugs they could find in their parents' medicine cabinets, such as left-over prescription painkillers. One night, Rachael shook me awake and said Michael seemed to be having a seizure and he was throwing up. It was terrifying, especially since I didn't know what he had taken and he didn't know what he had taken, either. He recovered after more vomiting and told me that he wouldn't attend one of those parties again.

About three months went by. One weekend night, I had a strong intuitive feeling that I needed to get in my car and go find Michael, even though it was only about nine thirty and he wasn't due home until eleven. I remember being asked why I was finding the car keys and getting ready to leave to look for Mike before his curfew. I said: "I'm not going to ignore my mother's intuition. I feel like Mike is in trouble." I drove to a park where the teenagers from his school liked to go and peered out my car window as I drove slowly past, searching for my son. I knew that Mike would probably find it really embarrassing if I showed up and he and his friends were just "hanging out," yet somehow I could sense that something was not right. Then I saw him walking aimlessly across the grass, alone. I opened the window and called to him, but he didn't even turn around to look at me. I got out of the car and crossed the lawn to where he was. When I got a few feet away, I could tell he was very drugged up and in trouble. His arms seemed to be bluish purple from the elbow down, and when I turned him to look at me, his eyes were vacant. He had no idea who I was. Terrified, I hooked my arm in his and half-dragged him toward the car, laid him across the backseat, and drove like a NASCAR driver to the nearest emergency room.

I knew this night was going to be one of the worst of my life, but I was also grateful that I had listened to my intuition and found my son. In the emergency room, Michael became very angry and tried to leave. He was shouting but unable to form any words. It took three male nurses to hold him down on the bed, and they finally had to put restraints on his wrists to keep him from pulling out the IVs. I stayed by his side as they drew blood and then administered charcoal tablets and water to absorb the drugs. After about thirty minutes, his arms returned to normal, and the attending doctor told me he was no longer in danger of dying but that he might have sustained kidney damage. There was nothing I could do except stay next to my son and pray.

After about two hours, Mike was able to recognize me and that he was in a hospital, but he was still belligerent and mostly incoherent. In my purse, I happened to have a small video camera I had used to tape my daughter's dance class earlier in the day. I decided to record this experience with Mike, because I wanted him to see, after he had recovered, what he had done to his mind and body. I got out the camera and started asking him simple questions like, "What are the names of your sisters?" and "What's your address?" He couldn't answer any of them. I began to panic that my son had permanently damaged his brain, but the doctor assured me that it was probably temporary until the drugs wore off completely.

Three hours later, Michael had recovered enough to hold a conversation with me. At first, he was defiant, telling me that he would have been fine and I shouldn't have searched him out. He was mad and wouldn't even look my way. I pulled my chair closer to his bed and pushed the PLAY button on the video camera. I knew it would have much more impact than anything I could tell him.

As he watched himself slur through words with glazed-over eyes, he started to cry. He covered his eyes and said, "Mom, I think I damaged my brain."

I put my hand on his arm and said, "Pray to God that you didn't and that you will be okay." Then he said, "I'm sorry, Mom," over and over again. It was heartbreaking, but I knew that night, for certain, that "sorry" wasn't going to last. My child had a drug problem. I knew I couldn't help him. He needed professional counseling. He had to go into a program.

While growing up, my brothers and I spent about 80 percent of every day in the company of at least one of our parents, either on tour, on a TV show, in a recording studio, or at home. We were certainly exposed to drugs and alcohol, but the fear of disappointing my parents was far stronger than any curiosity about drugs or alcohol. We were held accountable for our actions, and it was our responsibility to the rest of the group to do our best. There are many ways I could have benefited from having a more typical childhood, but this is one aspect I don't regret. I watched as my performing peers, especially my dear sweet friend Andy Gibb, sabotaged their health and their careers with drug use and, as in Andy's case, even died very young.

Back in the seventies and eighties, I don't think most people understood what kind of physical damage substance abuse causes to the brain and heart. But now there is no denying its negative effects. One study I heard of and looked up shows that the brains of young substance abusers are like those of patients with Alzheimer's disease (*Oxford Journal*, August 2010). Drug use burns out the natural neurotransmitter chemicals in your body that help produce joy and peace of mind. And there also seem to be more powerful and more addictive drugs available now than there were in the seventies.

As a mother who learned the hard way, I can tell you that there is no such thing as "experimenting" with drugs. Your child may tell you, "I only tried it once." Once is enough. Intervene. Monitor their friends and seek help for your child. Even if you don't understand drug use or aren't certain what's going on, step in to save your child. Don't write it off as them being sleepy or moody teenagers. At eighteen, Mike told me that he first started taking drugs when he was *twelve years old.* I had no idea. Be the parent. Let them know you're paying attention. Give them curfews, make sure you follow through, and try to stay up so that they know you're keeping track of the time. Trust me, having your child be embarrassed by you or angry with you for a year or two because you put limits on his social life is better than the alternative of your teenager becoming addicted or dying from drug use.

After doing some research, talking to professional counselors, and also seeking the advice of other parents, I sent Michael for six weeks to the Anasazi program of YoungWalkers. It's an amazing wilderness therapy program that combines psychology, nutrition, and physical challenges. The children go with highly trained counselors into the wilderness of Arizona to learn to live in nature, work as a team with their group, and communicate without the distractions of technology. They hike for miles every day, sleep on the ground in a sleeping bag, eat food they cook themselves over a campfire, and learn other great survival skills. The aim is for the teenager to understand that he has the power to make choices. The Anasazi program is also a great help for parents, who are fully involved with their child's program. I found that it gave me extremely helpful skills to communicate with all of my kids. It may not be the right program for every teenager, but my son seemed to thrive in it. He would always say that those were some of the best weeks of his life because he was challenged to grow and push himself beyond what he thought he could do.

He was a different boy when he came back home, centered,

calm, and more mature. He and I had long talks about what he had learned, his past struggles, and his new dreams. I could hear in his voice and with his new outlook on life the incredible adult that my son could have potentially become one day. He had learned great new skills, but there was a major stumbling block in his way. He was returning to the same household. Nothing had changed. I was still on an emotionally draining treadmill, working to support the whole family and feeling little peace of mind about my marriage. I know Michael sensed my hopelessness and even my loneliness. It's too much pressure for any child to worry about his mother's happiness. It robs him of his childhood. He isn't there yet, emotionally. We need to assure him that we are okay, that we are the adults and we can handle our problems.

In 2006, I found myself starting to struggle again with depression, which concerned me greatly because I never wanted to go back to that dark place I was in when I had postpartum depression. There are always factors that lead up to depression. This time, I had lost my mother, my father was rapidly declining in health, my older children were going through their teenage struggles, and I was trying to make wise career choices and still have time with my kids, to name just a few. I could feel myself spiraling deeper down as the responsibilities piled on. It was also exacerbated by severe female health issues that I had been experiencing for several years, which left me feeling generally lousy on a daily basis.

One late afternoon, as I was packing my bag to go to Philadelphia for several QVC shows, I became very concerned about flying because I was doubled over in pain. I couldn't imagine how I was even going to be able to leave the house, let alone get on a plane and fly for six hours. I called for a last-minute appointment with my doctor. In her office, I asked, "Will it be okay for me to fly out tomorrow morning? I really need to be on that plane, because these QVC shows are so difficult to rearrange. They are booked eight months in advance." I never expected her answer. She said, "Absolutely not! I'm scheduling you for emergency surgery in the morning." I drove home feeling even more despondent, not only about having major female surgery the next day, but also about having to disappoint my doll company, the QVC producers, and especially the thousands of viewers who always tuned in for the shows. Also, I knew that having surgery would leave me unable to take care of my kids for a while. But I had no choice. I was already weak and tired and it seemed to me like surgery was going to be one more stressor on my exhausted system.

What became an even bigger struggle is that I had to follow up that surgery with various medications to balance my hormones, which I was told could take a substantial amount of time to get the levels just right. I was raised to rehearse until I got it right; let's just say that was one long, long rehearsal! Each day I struggled more and more just to focus enough to get through the most mundane tasks, but it didn't register with me until months later that I was no longer able to think clearly.

Another doctor I went to see suggested an antidepressant, which I didn't really want to take after my previous experience with PPD, but I finally resigned myself to the evidence that it was worth a try again. The one I was prescribed this time did help the extreme lows, but it also took away any high emotion, too. It gave me more of a flat, joyless feeling, like playing one note on a piano.

I couldn't fully admit it to myself at the time, but I know now that the depression was, in part, brought on by my unwillingness to face that I felt my marriage was a failure. I couldn't imagine going through a second divorce, especially since I was the first person in my entire family who had ever been divorced even once. I dreaded having to hear or read the harsh public opinion I had endured following my first divorce. I also had to consider more than my own feelings. How would divorce affect my children, because there was a strong possibility it would be written about in magazines and become a topic of gossip on the Internet? Other students at my children's schools had made remarks to them in the past about having Marie Osmond as their mother, which was already difficult enough. I spent a lot of time on my knees, praying that my feelings would be resolved, asking that my family could just be happy. In retrospect, I thought it was the right thing to pray for because I was constantly being persuaded that staying in my marriage was what God wanted, "for better or for worse." With my busy life, I was rarely given one second alone even to think about it. So when my intuition, the whisperings of the spirit, would rise up through my consciousness to tell me that I needed to leave my marriage, I continually ignored it. I wanted God to fix it. But God won't take away our free will or agency. God can give us the promptings and direction, but then we have to listen and be proactive in fixing it for ourselves.

While trying to make sense of my feelings and struggling along physically for months following my surgery, I ended up in such a mental haze that I finally hit an all-time low. One afternoon, following yet another sleepless night and many other stressors I was dealing with on a daily basis, I was left completely broken-down, in pieces, and my emotions plummeted to the bottom until I felt no self-worth whatsoever. I went upstairs into the bathroom to try to collect myself. I remember thinking that I should take some of my medications to help me. That was my first mistake and also my last moment of any clarity. I don't remember much after that thought, but I was told later that I took more than I realized. It's all a blur to me, even now. My powers of reasoning and any logical thinking ability had diminished greatly, as if my brain had gone into shock from the emotional and physical pain. But my will to live must have remembered who I was and what had happened, because from somewhere deep inside of me a gleam of light arose through the dark mental haze. I must have sensed that I had to get help fast. I was told later I stumbled out into the hallway, calling for help, and then I passed out.

When I regained consciousness, I was in a hospital room and very confused as to how I had ended up there. I stayed for a few days while the doctors determined that the mixture of prescribed hormones I was taking following the surgical menopause, the antidepressant, and my thyroid medication were interacting in a very detrimental way that most likely started my emotional and physical downward spiral. They couldn't imagine how I had been able to function at all. I remember sitting in that hospital bed feeling like a complete failure. I was so unbelievably sad at what was going on in my life and how emotionally dead and physically drained I had become, I couldn't even recognize myself. I felt so alone.

While I was there, I talked to a counselor about some of the stress factors in my life, though I didn't bring up my internal conflict about wanting a divorce. It was still good for me to get perspective from an unbiased person and talk about the other issues going on in my life. But it would have helped more if I could have been completely open about everything. I wanted to, but I was still worried about my children's and my own privacy.

I had to take a long look at why I had let myself get to this place and whom I could trust to make sure it didn't happen again. What I finally came to realize is that I had to take care of myself. Grandmother Osmond was right when she told me as a child, "No one's going to take care of you but you. So you better learn how to do it, young lady." I think I'm finally learning how, Grandma.

At this point in my life, I choose a much healthier lifestyle and incorporate natural healing modalities, I eat foods that are good for my body when possible and exercise regularly, and I strive never to ignore my intuition. And importantly, I listen to its direction so that I can consciously choose joy.

I am writing about this difficult part of my life for two reasons.

First, it's imperative to remember that medication is medication and doctors are human beings. Medical professionals prescribe medicine that they believe will help, but they can

only make their best-educated choice, and this is tricky with antidepressants, especially when mixed with other medications you might be taking. One that seems to work well for other people may not work for you at all. The problem is, you may be too depressed to monitor your own reactions. Be sure to always schedule a follow-up appointment so the doctor can assess whether you are reacting in a positive manner to the prescribed medications. As a strong backup, ask your family members and close friends to keep a watch on any reactions you might have that don't seem to be for the better.

Also, get one of those weekly pillboxes to help you keep track of when you should take the medication. You have enough to think about when you are struggling without wondering if you took your medication or not. Also, more and more research is coming to the forefront that many kinds of prescribed and even over-the-counter medicines, if mixed incorrectly, can have mental and emotional side effects you may have never considered. The number of emergency room visits by people who mixed over-the-counter drugs to bad effect has more than doubled since 2004. It can't be stressed enough that if you're sick and in pain, you already aren't thinking clearly. Ongoing pain, whether physical or mental, begins to deactivate the frontal lobe of the brain, which is the part of the brain that helps you reason and make good decisions in the moment.

If you need to be on an antidepressant, you might want to see a therapist or some type of counselor as well. There is a reason you have depression that is creating your inability to function. The medication can give you a good base from which to start working on your problems, but unless you actually do work through those problems and make changes, the medication will only postpone your dealing with the true underlying issues. I know I finally had to ask myself, "Why am I trying to medicate instead of fix?" A great counselor opened my eyes to the basis of my question. She told me, "You're a 'fixer,' and you have a classic 'child-star' syndrome. You will do whatever is needed to accomplish what you must, because your goal has always been to make those around you happy. And now you are beginning to understand that you've done this at the expense of your own emotional and physical health." But she added, "It's not just child performers. It's the same issue for many, many women everywhere who were rewarded for being pleasers as girls. These girls, who usually suffer low self-esteem because of past issues, may confuse being controlled [by someone] with being taken care of." As she said these words, I knew that they applied to me and that they were truth.

Second: Love yourself enough to know that as a woman, and especially as a mother, you have to take care of yourself first, before you can take care of others. We can get swept up in tornadoes of activity, trying to conquer the storms in our lives. Instead, I've had to learn for myself that I need to go to the eye of the storm, the quiet center, to be able to see clearly and get perspective on why everything is spinning out of control around me. This usually means really taking the time to try to still your mind and listen to your intuition. For most women I know, as it was for me, this seems like a selfish approach to life. We can get caught in the trap of feeling guilty about not putting the needs of our children, our husbands, or even our employees or boss before our own. It's not true that it's "selfish." It's called "self-love." It took me two crises to accept that ignoring my intuition and suppressing what I knew to be true for myself only resulted in a drawn-out and painful process for myself and for my children as well. The biblical golden rule directs us: "Love your neighbor as yourself." What I forgot about that powerful scripture is the part about loving "yourself." You have to love yourself to truly know how to love others. It's how you learn to love.

Children need a healthy mother to create a healthy home. The airplane-emergency metaphor holds a deep truth: "First put on your oxygen mask and then assist your child." I once asked an airline attendant why this was the direction. She told me that if the airplane ever lost altitude quickly, it would only take seven to fifteen seconds to lose consciousness. Obviously, if you have blacked out, your ability to help your kids is zero.

When it comes to looking back, clarity is painful, but it is the only way to healing. It takes forgiveness, as well. I wish so much that my sweet Michael had been able to give himself the chance to look back to see with the clarity that only comes with some time.

Michael went through another rehab program in the fall of 2007. It was leaked to the tabloids about a week after my divorce papers had been signed and while I was commuting from my Utah home to LA to be on *Dancing with the Stars*. I felt devastated and worried that Mike had to have his private life revealed to the public. Somehow, my son found out about the tabloid report and was horribly humiliated. I missed two rehearsals to go to be with my son. We talked for hours, through the night. He said he wasn't sure he could ever deal with some of his problems, but he promised that he would try. The hardest thing for me to do was to go back and finish my weeks on *Dancing with the Stars*. Learning the quickstep seemed so trivial, considering that my son was in pain. My mother would always tell me, "A mother is only as happy as her least happy child." And she was right. I had to strive to appear happy on almost every show. I would drop to my knees and pray that God would see me through. All I wanted to do was call it quits and gather my kids around me, but I had to follow through on my commitment to my contract with the show. I managed to smile, but my heart was splintering day by day in my chest. One of the obligations of making it into the finals on the show was that all three couples were to fly to New York and appear on *Good Morning America* the next day. The producers gracefully let me out of that red-eye plane trip and appearance so that I could be with my son again following the competition.

A mallard duck will return to the same territory year after year.

My son had a couple of clean and hope-filled months in early 2008, after his release from his rehab program. I was so happy to have him back home with me. He found a job that spring with a music event planner. One afternoon he was working to lift trusses and hang lights and pulled the muscles in his back. A coworker drove him to a doctor, who checked him out and sent him away with a prescription for painkillers. He filled the prescription before I could even get home that evening. I took them away from him, but he had already taken two. That was all it took. A month later, I could tell my son was hooked on prescription medications and had found ways to get them. My brothers and I were committed to doing an Osmond fiftieth anniversary tour to sold-out venues across the UK and some of Asia. They had already included my name in all of the advertising. Mike was going to go with me to help out onstage and to keep an eye on the younger children, but I knew in my heart I couldn't have him go. One afternoon, I arranged for a rehab center to pick up my son at one of our rehearsals. I had a strong feeling that he would run away if he thought I knew he was using drugs again. Crying, I gathered all of my brothers before the rehearsal and asked them to help me. When Mike walked into rehearsal that afternoon, all eight of my brothers formed a circle around him. Mike knew instantly what was going on, but he respected his uncles enough to not fight his way out of the circle.

One of my brothers spoke for the rest. "Michael, you're our nephew. We love you, but you are lying to your mother about your addictions. We know that you're using drugs again. We all want you to get better. You're not going to be going on tour with us. You're going back to rehab today. There is a car here waiting to take you."

I could see the anger in my son's eyes as I hugged him good-bye. He didn't hug me back. I wasn't sure how I was going to leave, but I knew he would be safe. I wouldn't have been able to protect him if he had gone with us. There would be too much danger with so many opportunities and so many strangers around who could possibly facilitate his addictions. My daughter Rachael offered to stay home from the tour to be close by for Michael, and I checked in daily by phone from the road. Every day, the news of progress seemed better and better, which made it a little bit easier for me to be away. After a couple of weeks out of the country, I returned to a son who looked so much more like the healthy boy I had known. He was working out with free weights, studying with a tutor, and talking to a great counselor he had there.

A few months later, Donny and I performed a limited-run show at the MGM Grand Hotel in Las Vegas. With the overwhelming success of that show, we were offered a two-year run at the Flamingo Hotel. It was a change that I was ready to make. My life in Utah had run its course, and since both of my parents had passed away by then, I had no strong reason to stay.

When I was growing up, we would always have a family meeting to discuss big life changes that would affect the whole family, like moving to a new location or home. Every family member was allowed to cast a vote as to whether they thought it was a good idea. In the same way, I held a family meeting about moving to Las Vegas with the kids. There wasn't one "nay" vote in the bunch. Everyone wanted a fresh start. The older kids were done with high school, except for Michael. Jessica and Stephen were already out of the house, with apartments of their own, and Rachael wanted to work on the Vegas show, so she was happy about the move. The younger four were nervous but excited about the change and living in a whole new area.

Michael was finishing his rehab program in Utah, and when I visited him there one day to get his opinion about relocating to Las Vegas, he made a mature plea to me.

He told me that he wanted to finish his high school education in a real school and not get a GED in the rehab program. I conferred with his counselors, and they felt that Mike would soon be ready to go home anyway. Michael made a promise to me that if I even suspected him of ever doing drugs again I could kick him out of the house and he would live with the consequences of being on his own. It was something we never even had to contemplate because my son made good on his promise.

When choosing a nesting site, mallards are very careful. They know how important it is to find a place that is safe from predators.

At age seventeen, Michael came home to become the "man of the family." He flew to Vegas to help me pick out a house for us to rent until we decided where we would buy. After a full day of looking, we both agreed on the same one, a house in a Vegas suburb about twenty minutes from the Flamingo Hotel, where our show was. When Michael and I opened the door with my key to the new place, I was overwhelmed with something I had not felt in twenty years. I was free! I was free in a home that I looked forward to making my own, for me and my kids.

Despite the stress that came with moving and starting a new show at the Flamingo, I loved it all, and so did Michael and the other kids. I rented a U-Haul trailer to pull behind the car for the move from Utah to Las Vegas. I told the kids, "Whatever fits in this trailer is what moves with us, so only bring your favorite toys, sports equipment, clothes, books, and things you would miss." My ex-husband decided he wanted to keep the Utah house and so most of the furniture stayed. I packed some cookware, a big-screen TV for our family room, some furniture that had been passed down from my mother and grandmother, and my favorite books and works of art, which I had collected over the years, including my rare dolls from my collection.

With the help of a couple of my close girlfriends and Rachael, we drove two cars, one towing the trailer, to the new house in Las Vegas. We arrived after midnight and, exhausted, camped out on the floor of one of the kids' bedrooms on blow-up mattresses. Listening to their sleepy voices talking about how they wanted to set up their bedrooms and how cool the new house was going to be for having birthday parties made me feel so happy and comforted to my core. I knew I had made a wise choice. The next morning, we unloaded the U-Haul before everything baked in the July sun, and took off to the furniture discounters to buy new furniture for our house.

Mike had brought with him his favorite futon couch for his room, but I insisted he have a regular bed as well. The room that we converted into his bedroom was originally a recreation room that came with a sink and a refrigerator. Mike loved this room. It was like his bachelor den, and everything about it made him smile.

He was always the tidiest of my kids, even as a young child. When we were on tour, he would line up his toys on the edge of the bus window. At around age eight, he started collecting exotic insect specimens, from metallic beetles to Malaysian water bugs, which had been preserved and mounted in various shadow boxes. He was fascinated by the bugs' intricate eyes, their fuzzy pinchers, and the patterns in the design of their wings. You've never seen a more artistic display of something so nasty. I was just grateful that they were no longer moving around.

Now, in this room to call his own, he was thrilled to have a refrigerator in which he could keep a carton of juice that no one else had drunk out of without pouring it into a glass. His room was always the only one that was kept in immaculate form. Whenever I would feel overwhelmed by the clutter of four kids under age twelve, I would go and sit in Michael's room for a bit. His guaranteed neatness would always calm my mind. Mike applied to a performing arts high school in Las Vegas and was accepted for his musical skills, but then he decided that a regular public high school would be better. Even though he loved music, he never thought about making a living as a musician. His first love was textiles, design, and fashion marketing.

It's not easy to be the "new kid" for your senior year of high school, living in a new city, and focusing on staying clean every single day. He also got a job at a frozen yogurt store. He thought he would be running the register, but he was relegated to mopping the floors, wiping down tables, and sanitizing the handles on the machines. It was humbling, but he told me that it made him really think about how many things go into keeping a business running. Interestingly, he started helping out at home more often, too, doing household chores without having to be asked. He became an excellent influence on the younger kids, often helping them with homework, playing with them in the pool, guiding them through their chores, and even reprimanding them if they spoke to me in a sassy tone of voice.

His next job was at a very trendy clothing store in the Forum Shops at Caesars Palace. He saved his paychecks, only using some of the money to buy clothes to wear to work. On his own, Michael decided that if he was going to have a career in design, he needed to learn to sew. A friend of mine who is an excellent seamstress offered to start Mike off with the basics. Michael went to her home once a week, carrying one of my smaller sewing machines in a case, and worked on a project with her. He never missed a week, unless he was sick. I loved the huge smile on his face when he came home the very first week, showing me the pillowcase he made with perfectly straight seams.

Halfway through his senior year, Michael got in contact with FIDM (Fashion Institute of Design and Merchandising) in Los Angeles through an inspiring guidance counselor, Gina.

With Gina's encouragement, Michael completed all of the applications and the entry projects, letters of recommendation, and portfolio work needed to apply for admission. In his college entrance essay, Mike wrote: "College hasn't been a goal for me my whole life. I actually laughed at the idea of college until I became a stagehand, setting up the sound, video, and lighting for music groups. I had to lift 200-pound trusses, which is basically a big hunk of metal that holds lights. That's when I decided that I should do something better with my life. I thought about what I would do if I could wave a magic wand and become anything I wanted. I wanted to become a world-class clothing designer."

On his eighteenth birthday, Michael and I flew to Los Angeles for his interview with the director of admissions. We talked in the car from the airport to the school as a way to rehearse how he would express his hopes and goals for his college career. He was amazingly eloquent, charming, funny, and focused, and they decided to accept him on the spot.

I sat next to this darling young man and realized all he had accomplished in one year and all by his own willpower. He was graduating from high school with a 3.9 GPA, had held three jobs, passed a driver's test, and gotten his license, initiated his research into higher education, applied for the college he wanted to attend, and collected all the letters of recommendation, and here we were, with his dreams on the verge of becoming a reality. And, through all of it, Michael had stayed away from drugs. My son was a remarkable boy and on his way to becoming an incredible man.

*Most male ducks are silent and would rather be left
undisturbed.*

Las Vegas had been a fresh start for Michael, and with one
successful, drug-free year behind him, he felt he was ready for
the challenge that college would bring. He couldn't wait to
delve into the life he wanted more than anything. As he wrote
in his application essay: "My mind is full of ideas that I can't
wait to express with a pencil and a piece of paper. I feel like
that newly born bird that wants to fly with all its heart and is
trying to find the courage. I am excited to experience the life I
can have, if I just stay focused."

Before he left for college, Michael cleaned out his bedroom
so that it could be used as a guest room while he was gone. As
we were packing, he told me a lot I didn't know about how
he'd felt growing up. It's impossible to rewrite history; so I
practice forgiving myself for not seeing clearly what was creating pain for my son. Children don't have the life experience to
judge their circumstances. Other mothers have told me the
same: "I can't believe my child didn't tell me what was going
on." This is exactly why, as mothers, we have to be so diligent
in reminding our children that they can tell us anything they
want without fear that we will be angry. We need to remind
our children, occasionally and without frightening them, that
if something happens that feels wrong or hurtful, then they
need to come and tell us, even if it points the finger at someone
they see as your friend or a member of their family.

My son said that a few years earlier he had asked my father, his beloved grandpa, for advice about possibly changing his last name. His grandpa told him about his own childhood: how after his father had died when he was an infant he had had two different stepfathers, who were both extremely difficult. He said to Mike, "Son, you must forgive and move on. But you also must be able to live with honor for your name. If that can't be done with the name you carry now, then change it for your own peace of mind." In the same words he used for each of his own nine children while we were growing up, my father told Michael, "There are two things worth defending to the death: your faith in God and your good name." As we finished packing his room, Mike told me that he planned to sever ties with his father completely and change his last name to Bryan, which was his middle name. He felt that Michael Bryan also had a better ring for a designer. I won't write about my son's reasons for wanting to change his name for the sake of privacy. It was a legal privilege that he looked forward to when he turned eighteen.

A group of Mallards can be called a raft or a team.

During Michael's first semester of college, I was working as a correspondent for *Entertainment Tonight* covering *Dancing with the Stars*. It was the season that Donny was one of the celebrity contestants (and, in case you haven't heard *on every* show he's done since then, yes, he won). Every Monday morning for ten weeks, I flew to Los Angeles from Las Vegas for the shows that taped and aired on Monday and Tuesday. I would pick up Michael after his morning class on Mondays, and we would spend most of the day together and then have dinner after the show was done taping. He would then stay with me at whatever hotel I was in, and we would sit up and talk until about two a.m. The next morning, we would have breakfast, run errands for school supplies, or whatever he needed. Then I would drop him off for his afternoon class, go to the show, and fly home that evening. I loved having these hours with my son and hearing about his life at school, meeting his new friends in his apartment building, and looking at his finished creative assignments. Often we would get tacos at his favorite place and then try to walk them off on the beach. He would tell me about the girl he was interested in dating and why he was attracted to her, and ask my advice about asking her out. I was just starting to date Steve again, so I could sympathize. I was feeling pretty much like an awkward eighteen-year-old, too. During one of our long walks on the beach, my son turned to me and said, "Mom, I really like Steve. And I want you to be happy. If you ever want to marry him again, you have my approval."

I knew Michael was being sincere. I also know he could tell that Steve was making me happy and that he was a good father figure for his younger siblings. He could also see how Steve was willing to put the effort into helping me as a mother. After all, it was Steve who was there to carry boxes when Michael moved into his new apartment and to help him set it up with everything my son might need. I think many mothers experience a rather sweet turning point with a grown child, though it usually can't be linked to a specific day. It's more of a gradual change of perception, when your child becomes aware that you are more than a mom. You are a woman who deserves happiness of her own.

When Michael came home for the holidays, he seemed to be even more aware of his status as an adult, especially to his younger siblings. He would spend hours riding skateboards and playing football with the boys and trying to teach Abigail to ride a two-wheeled bike. There was only one present on his wish list: a printer so he could print out his assignments in his apartment. When I asked what gift he wanted for fun, he said, "Things don't matter to me, Mom. I just want to find a wife, have a family, and travel the world whenever we can."

After the Christmas break, when he was back at school, I flew to Los Angeles for a scheduled TV interview with Mary Hart of *Entertainment Tonight*, and Mike came with me. Mary always asked about each of my kids, and when she saw Michael, she enthusiastically asked him about FIDM.

Mike answered, "I've never been happier."

The week my son passed away, a friend from his drug-taking days decided to pay Michael a visit, arriving with some of her other friends in tow. Michael's roommate told us later that this group wanted to go out to experience Los Angeles, and Mike was asked to be the designated driver as they were intending to drink and they thought they might end up intoxicated by the end of the evening. Not wanting to be rude, Michael agreed to go out with them. We were told that the next morning, about seven a.m., Mike returned to the apartment, alone and looking terrible. He told his roommate that he had woken up under a highway overpass and had walked back home. He had no idea where his friends had gone, how he had gotten there, or what had happened along the way, only that they had obviously left him. He said he had not had any alcohol or taken any drugs on his own, but felt that one of the people in the car must have laced what he was drinking with something that made him pass out. According to his roommate, Mike missed his classes that day and the next day, too, and could barely manage to get out of bed the following evening. This all happened just a few days before he passed away.

Michael never told me of this incident, but my mother's intuition was telling me two days before he died that something was different. I heard a change in his voice over the phone, and it frightened me. He sounded weary and disappointed and said that he felt like he had no friends, even though his roommate and his new best female friend at school both assured me that Michael was always with their group of friends and rarely spent an evening alone. I could hear that he was emotionally down, but I thought it was compounded by the stress of finals. I also wondered if he had been turned down by one of the girls he was interested in dating and didn't want to tell me about it. I later found out that he was using a prescription medicine for his acne that has now been shown to raise the risk of depression in some people. Parents, you must research any and all prescribed drugs, even if it's to treat something as minor as acne.

I know now, too late, that my son was masking how deeply depressed he was.

I had three more shows at the Flamingo that week and a speaking engagement at a luncheon for five hundred business-women the next day, so I told Mike I would get him a plane ticket and he should come to Vegas to be with his brothers and sisters for a couple of days, but he didn't want to miss any more classes. In that case, I said, I would fly to LA on Monday, my day off, and we would go to lunch and talk about what was going on. We spoke a little longer, and we left the conversation with our plans made.

I've gone over that phone conversation thousands of times in my memory. What could I have possibly said differently? What if I had known that it would be the last time I spoke to my son? My one consolation is that I never end a conversation with any of my children without saying, "I love you." It was the last thing I said to my son.

Ducks' feet have no nerves or blood vessels. This means ducks never feel the cold, even if they swim in icy cold water.

My daughter Rachael, who works on our Vegas show as a costume designer and my wardrobe assistant, was the closest in age to Michael. When he left for college, she missed him greatly, and they would talk on the phone a couple of times every day. That Friday, I sent Mike two text messages telling him to check in with me, but he didn't respond. Then, during a costume change about twenty minutes into the Vegas show, my makeup person, Kim, looked at the caller ID on my phone and said, "Michael called while you were onstage." I was relieved at hearing from him and thought that he must have been okay. I assumed that he had left a message and I would call him back right after the show. He didn't leave a message.

Rachael told me later that he called her cell phone during the middle of the show. She picked it up long enough to say, "Hi," and said that she'd have to call him back, because everyone was hurrying to get costumes ready for the next quick change. She could tell by his voice that something was wrong, though, so she stopped long enough to ask him about it. "You sound down. What's going on?"

He answered, "I just haven't felt good." Then he told her, "I love you. No matter what happens, I will always love you. You need to promise me something. Don't marry the guy you are dating right now. He's not the one for you."

"I'll call you back in a bit," Rachael said. "You're okay?"

"Yes. I'll be fine," Michael responded.

When Rachael tried him back about twenty minutes later, Mike didn't answer his phone.

My executive assistant's youngest daughter had gotten married earlier in the day, so after the show and the "Meet 'n Greet," Rachael and I and members of my executive assistant's family gathered in my dressing room so they could fill us in on the highlights of the wedding. Before I started chatting with them, I called Michael. He didn't answer. About ten minutes later, Rachael tried to reach Mike on her phone and again got no answer, so we both thought that he had gone to sleep or was with friends.

I didn't have to hurry home that night because all four of the younger kids had gone to Utah to stay with my brother Jimmy and sister-in-law Michelle. Jimmy's youngest daughter was being baptized the next morning, and the kids all wanted to be there to celebrate. Steve offered to drive them to Utah because he had some business there and also wanted to see our son, Stephen.

I was exhausted from a nonstop week with the shows and the luncheon speech the previous day, and I was supposed to be back at the Flamingo the next day pretty early for a costume fitting. Donny had flown home in his personal plane to spend the day with his family and would be returning before the Saturday show.

For some reason, which I thought was exhaustion, I felt like I couldn't go home to an empty house, so I decided to stay the night in a hotel room at the Flamingo. I asked Rachael to stay with me overnight, telling her that I needed her. On any other night, Rachael might have laughed and said she was going to her own apartment, but this night she agreed immediately. Looking back, we must have sensed that we would need to be with each other more than we could ever have imagined.

We finally got into a hotel room, and I was getting ready for bed about one a.m., after checking my phone again and listening to messages from the younger kids. Rachael had crawled into bed and was already asleep when my cell phone rang around one thirty a.m. I didn't recognize the number, so I let it go to voice mail. No one left a message. This happened again, and finally, the third time the number rang, I decided to pick it up. I was sure it was a wrong number.

The person on the other end was the guard at the gate that leads into my neighborhood. He told me that there was a police officer there to talk to me and asked if it was okay for him to let him through to my house. I said, "I'm not there. I'm at the Flamingo Hotel. What's this about?" The security guard said, "They won't tell me, except someone is here from the coroner's office. They are coming to the Flamingo to see you."

My heart dropped to the floor, but my head went into instant denial. I kept telling myself that this was some type of mistake. Rachael sat up in bed, wide-awake, when she heard me on the phone. After I hung up, my legs started shaking uncontrollably. I said to Rachael, "It's Mike. It has to be Michael."

"No, Mom, no," she said. "I'll reach him. I'll call right now." She dialed and redialed Michael's cell phone, over and over. She kept saying, "Pick up, Michael. Come on. Be there."

I called the friends whose daughter's wedding we had been celebrating. They were staying at the hotel, too. I told them about the phone call and asked them to please be with Rachael and me when the officer got there. They came right away to our room. I don't remember what we talked about or how long it took for the officers to arrive. My pulse was pounding in my ears, and Rachael and I were trying to think of someone to call at Mike's school, but were hesitating; it was now two a.m. and we didn't want to alarm anyone for no reason.

One of my friends opened the hotel room door for the officers. After they identified me, the officer from the coroner's office said, "I'm very sorry to inform you that your son Michael committed suicide at nine twenty-five this evening."

When he left, he turned at the door to say once again, "I'm very, very sorry."

The next thing I remember is seeing Rachael on her knees with her face in her hands. Her legs had collapsed beneath her. I thought, How can I comfort my daughter when I can't even catch my own breath? I thought someone had run a knife into my heart. It was the worst stab of pain I've ever felt. I tried to wake myself up from the nightmare, because this news couldn't have been true. My own legs started to shake uncontrollably.

My friends must have carried us over to sit on the bed. Rachael fell into my arms. The rest became a blur for at least an hour. I was unable to even speak without hyperventilating, so as soon as Rachael was able, she called Stephen and Jessica.

I don't know how she had the strength, but that is my daughter. She has never fallen apart on me when I needed her most.

At some point my friends called their oldest son, who was attending law school in LA. They were concerned that the paparazzi would soon be on the scene at the apartment building where Michael had lived. They asked their son, who was married, had a newborn at home, and was studying for his bar exam, to go and gather up Mike's belongings so that nothing would be lost or taken in all the confusion. In an ultimate act of kindness, not only did their son get everything from Mike's apartment that belonged to him—he also drove it the four hours to Las Vegas, in the middle of the night, so that I would have it at home and there would be no tabloid photos of his belongings being removed.

Then I called Steve. I had to have my babies come home to be with me. I wanted to hold them all in my arms so badly, even though I had no idea how I was going to be able to tell them what had happened. Steve was so upset that he was speechless at first, but he promised me he would bring all the kids back to Las Vegas as soon as he could arrange it. He ended up driving them through the night to be with me. When they would wake up from dozing in the car and wanted to know what was wrong, Steve just said, "Your mom needs you tonight."

When Donny got the news, he did what my family always does in a crisis. He rallied my brothers and said, "Our sister needs us. Meet me at the Provo airport in two hours." Virl, Merrill, Jay, and Jimmy got ready to go with Donny. The other brothers lived too far away to make it to the airport. Jimmy told me later, "Even though it was my daughter's baptism party, I couldn't celebrate her life knowing you had lost your child."

We had to call and wake my publicist, Alan Nierob, to help buffer the press once the news was out, which happened quickly. He was amazing in his response and very comforting. He began fielding phone calls that were coming and took immediate steps to deflect the paparazzi from invading the privacy of my kids.

Sometime after four a.m., my friends drove me to the house. I was exhausted and lay down on my bed and somehow managed to doze off for a bit while waiting for my brothers to arrive. I fell into a dream state that seemed so real. I saw my mother walk up to Michael, who was standing alone. She cradled the left side of his face in her hand and asked, "Are you okay?" Michael nodded yes. Then she said, "Do you know where you are?" and Michael said yes. Then my sweet mother said, "Come with me now."

In my dream, she took Mike's hand and led him away. She was taking care of him. My little boy was safe with his grandma.

My tears woke me up. At first I couldn't figure out if it was a dream or if I had really seen my son, and for a very brief moment, I actually forgot what had happened. Then the pain came back fully, but with a different intensity, because after the dream, there was an odd feeling of peace that surrounded the massive heartache.

I won't write about when my little ones arrived home or how I told them about what had happened. My kids will forever have their own memories of that day and their own ways to process losing their brother. I want them to have their privacy about it. For the next two days, we stayed together, all in the same room, shedding many tears, sharing sweet stories, and riding out the relentless tsunami waves of grief.

My next memory is when my brothers arrived, and my little family and I sobbed in their arms until no more tears could be shed for a while. Being men of great faith, they gathered around me to offer up a prayer of comfort and blessings. There is no better path to healing for me than to have my faith that my family could lay this burden in the care of a loving Father in

Heaven's arms and His beloved son, Jesus Christ, who not only atoned for our sins but for our deepest sorrows. I could feel to my core that He would sustain my family and me through the sad days ahead. Shortly after this, my friend's son arrived by car from Los Angeles with all of Michael's possessions, which were carried into my bedroom. I thanked him for sparing me the heartache of gathering his belongings myself, especially under the spotlight of the press. He wanted me to be aware of one thing he had found that he felt I should know about before anyone else. When he had entered Michael's bedroom, he found a legal form open on the floor in front of my son's backpack. It had been filled out, signed, and dated by Mike. It was the form to have his last name legally changed to Bryan. I know Michael left it there to be certain that it would be found and not overlooked, no matter what. He knew that his brothers and sisters and I would make sure to follow through for him on his wishes. My friend's son had folded it up and put it in Michael's backpack to bring to me. How blessed I was to have my friends with me and to be able to have my son's privacy protected as much as possible.

I knew I wouldn't be able to look at my son's other belongings right then, so I went into the bathroom to wash my face and comb my hair. I didn't want my younger children to be even more concerned, seeing how awful I looked, my face swollen and blotchy from crying. As I was running a brush through my hair, I had a powerful feeling that I was being directed to look through a certain box that had been brought from Mike's apartment; I had a strong sense that he didn't want it left where his younger brothers and sisters might find it. I opened it to find Mike's collection of CDs. I looked through the CD case and found quite a bit of music that I would never allow the younger kids to have. In a strange way, it gave me a sense of comfort that Mike might have directed me to his CD case to protect his siblings. It's something he would have done.

After two days of family time, it was time to go to Utah to arrange for my son's funeral with Jessica, Rachael, and Stephen. My son's body was being transported from Los Angeles to a mortuary there, and Steve offered to drive me.

It was tough to leave my younger kids for a couple of days, but I knew that they were in loving hands with one of my best friends, who is like an aunt to my kids and provided the comfort that they needed, making toasted sandwiches, reading books, and playing board games. A day later, my oldest friend, Patty, who is also like an aunt to my babies, arrived to help ease the burden.

We left, with Jessica, at about eight p.m. We wanted to leave in the dark and arrive while it was still dark, because we had word that paparazzi were waiting to catch me leaving my neighborhood. Rachael rode with Stephen and had left earlier in the day.

Jessica had spent the last two days living up to her nickname "Angelic" from the moment she arrived at the house: getting meals organized, reminding me of phone calls that needed to be made, and bringing the serenity of routine back to the kids. She was now exhausted and slept on the backseat of Steve's car the entire trip back to Utah. Steve and I talked for hours about what to do with the information we had about Michael's death.

Some of the people who knew and loved Michael thought that we should have the police track down the kids he was with the night he woke up under the overpass and started the downward spiral of depression. Some advised us to have them questioned and possibly prosecuted, especially since Mike's cell phone contained text messages from one of them saying, "I'm sorry, Mike. We didn't know." I prayed long and hard about what to do. Were they to blame for my son's death, or was it an impulsive and juvenile decision that went in a direction they could never have guessed? One investigator did speak to the young woman who had shown up with her friends to visit but felt he had no evidence that there had been any foul play that would result in death. A number of studies have shown that a majority of teenagers perceive themselves as invincible and feel that they can get away with all kinds of dangerous behavior, which is most likely the reason the death rate from car accidents involving teenagers is so high. Especially when it comes to drugs, teenagers rarely consider the repercussions of their actions. There was a lot of speculation in the media and on the Internet about whether drugs or alcohol were in Mike's system on the day he died. The autopsy and the toxicology report both showed that no illegal drugs were in his system. My son kept his promise to stay clean and sober, but he was suffering a personal Gethsemane that week about whatever simple drug was slipped to him the night he picked those kids up. I believe they had no idea what it would do to him physically, something he would never overcome. Depression kills the human spirit, and when it controls the mind, it can kill the body.

The harshest form of reality for a mother may be to see the corpse of her child. In my faith, I believe that the spirit continues on, even after we leave our earthly bodies. But to look at the face of my sweet son and have to accept that I would never see it on this earth again—I didn't know if I could stand it. Steve said a prayer for me in the car before we entered the building and then held my arm as the mortuary assistant led us to the room that held my sweet baby's body. Steve was concerned that this would be a horrible shock in my state of emotions, but God's grace prevailed over all worries and I felt a sense of peace and calm. I rested on my deep faith that day, just as I saw in my dream on the night Mike died that he was safe in the care of my mother's arms and those who have always loved him. After all, he had been born on her birthday. I couldn't imagine anybody more perfect to greet him than her.

As I looked at his face, I thought about being in this same room at the mortuary with my mother's body in 2004. A few days after my mother passed away, my daughters, a few close girlfriends, and I met at the mortuary to dress her body for the viewing before her memorial service. I applied my mother's makeup, and my dear friend and longtime hairdresser styled her hair just the way she loved it. I remember looking at my mom's face—which no longer showed the struggle or pain of her final six months on this earth. Her hands—which had held and nurtured so many children, sewn hundreds of shirts, dresses, and quilts, baked bread, prepared meals, carried suitcases, planted the garden, tended the sick, kept the budget books, written hundreds of personal letters and newsletters to our fans and thousands of pages of journals and recipes—were finally still, no longer busy with the work of this life. Her feet, which had danced to big band music with my father, walked the floor all night long as she soothed ailing babies and grand-babies, traveled the world with her performing family, stood up to wrongdoing, and walked in faith—those feet, which had been so swollen in her last weeks of life, had now returned to normal size. Her body had softened, no longer having to work around or through the aches and pains of aging bones, tired muscles, and a heart weakened by many strokes.

Right after she had passed away, I was standing at the foot of her bed, watching as the nurse removed my mother's feeding tube and IVs from her body. I had the distinct feeling that my mother was watching it happen as well, but not in a sad or regretful way. She was there in gratitude, thanking her body for supporting her and carrying her through seventy-nine years of life. It gave me a profound appreciation for the gift of our bodies.

Dressing my son for the viewing before his memorial service contained none of the grace-filled feeling I had had with my mother, even though his face did appear peaceful and free of emotional pain. I had an abiding feeling that Mike wanted me to know that he was sorry for putting me through this and also that he was at peace and feeling joy where he was. That did give me some comfort. But even though I clung to my faith that my son was fine and in Heavenly Father's care, my daughters and I still had to cope with the sight of his beautiful, healthy, young body which had been discarded in one moment of temporary insanity or irreversible impulse.

I only write these words hoping that they will be read by any person considering suicide as a way to spare your family more grief or because of a false perception that everyone would be better off without you. There is *nothing* better about life without you. There is no problem that isn't fixable, except for one: if you make a choice to kill yourself. There isn't a more hurtful way to leave your family behind. The physical ramifications to the body of any type of suicide are almost unbearably difficult for your family to see, especially your mother.

To look at the damage to my baby's body, and to know that there was absolutely nothing that I could do to make it better or different, was the worst kind of torture. Viewing Michael's bruised and broken body flooded me with memories that only another parent would understand. This was the baby boy I had held in my arms for hours, in awe of the miracle of being blessed with another son. He had been instantly imprinted on my heart and in my soul as my son forever. I had memorized the scent of his feathery hair and could have found him, blindfolded, in a room with hundreds of other babies. I knew the curve of his chin and the shell-like structure of his tiny ears. I adored the way his head tilted to one side when he was listening, the pomegranate red flush of his cheeks when he had been playing hard. I knew how his eyebrows gleamed in the sun when wet from the pool, the shape of his toes, and each place on his back that held a freckle or birthmark. I could predict the way his blue eyes would change in color depending on the shirt he was wearing. Protecting him and my other children from illness and accidents was one of my main concerns as a mother. Until the day he left home, I would go in his room to check on him when he was sleeping, pulling the quilt up over his curled-up body, just as I've always done for each of my kids. Every time I did, I would smile about his baby blanket, which he still had in a dresser drawer, and the way all my kids have kept theirs even into adulthood. Now, as I looked down at my son, the wave of grief pulled me under again, knowing that I would tuck his blanket over him for the last time in his coffin. It was going to be so hard to leave his side, yet I knew he was, in spirit, no longer there. No longer in pain, no longer depressed, no longer in conflict about the things that kept him unhappy. For that, I was grateful and I knew somehow God's grace would mend my shattered heart.

All of my brothers, their families, and many, many relatives, friends, and business associates attended my son's memorial service. Each of my children, except Jessica, who became too overcome when it was her turn to speak, wrote and read a eulogy to their brother. Rachael sang a song accompanied by one of my longtime friends and band members, and Stephen sang a song he had composed specifically for Michael. Everywhere you looked, there were beautiful flower arrangements, hundreds of them, sent by people I love and who knew how much I love my kids. I was touched so deeply by people in the entertainment community who reached out to my children and me with letters of sympathy, beautiful flowers and cards, or generous donations to Children's Miracle Network. To get warm messages from Oprah, the Jacksons, Bette Midler, Olivia Newton-John, Gladys Knight, Mary Hart, Barbara Walters, and Garth Brooks and Trisha Yearwood, and so many more friends I've worked with over the years reminded me how much show business is a "family" business, even if we may not see one another often. Flowers and cards arrived from hundreds of Children's Miracle Network connections. Two large boxes of cards arrived from all of the Paul Mitchell school students and customers who raise thousands of dollars for Children's Miracle Network. However, I think I was most emotionally overwhelmed by the thousands of cards from people around the world who just wanted to send us their love, some of whom shared with me their own story of tragic loss and ways to cope. I have kept every card in a large chest. I know that one day my children may want to see them all again. At the end of each day, when my heart would be breaking all over again, I would stop to remember, in gratitude, how blessed I am to have so many people who thought about and prayed for my family during that time. I know those prayers strengthened my faith and carried me through. I truly understand the power of prayer.

It was the power of prayer that sustained me to return to the *Donny & Marie Show* at the Flamingo the day after Michael's funeral. I know many of my friends thought it was too soon to go back to work, and I heard that there were many criticisms of my choice from the public. But I have to tell you, I prayed about it a lot to discern what would be the best thing to do for the children and for me. My perspective on every aspect of my life had shifted. What seemed a burden to me before no longer mattered; other things seemed way too light and trivial in the lonely light of losing a child. I became very concerned that if I didn't go back to a regular routine, I would never want to appear in public again. My emotional side wanted to hole up in the house with my children, close the blinds, unplug the Internet, and just dwell in our sadness. My younger children were already telling me that they felt they couldn't go back to school and face everyone's sympathy or their questions or remarks. They would cry and ask me how life would ever be normal again. The answer to my prayer was for me to lead the way for my family. I had to show my children that we had to continue on as a family. It's the only way.

The first night, it took all I had to make it through the show. I would get through a number, run offstage for a costume change, and fight back the tears. There was my solo section of the show, which I closed with *"Pie Jesu,"* a challenging operatic-style requiem that I sang from an elevated platform on the stage. At the end of the song, the platform descends behind curtains in billowing fog. I somehow made it through the song, but as most singers will tell you, singing in that style resonates with every emotion and brings them to the surface. By the time the platform reached the backstage floor, my legs had gone out from under me and I had collapsed, staring at the blurry stage lights above me. I couldn't breathe from the sorrow and started to hyperventilate. Rachael and one of the backstage crew literally had to prop me up between them to get me to my dressing room.

I lay on the couch in my dressing room as Donny went on-stage to perform his solo section. My heart was in so much pain, I thought that if I only closed my eyes and relaxed, I would die. Nothing mattered to me. My business manager and the show producer were standing nearby, and I told them that I was done, that it was impossible for me to ever do another show.

Rachael took my forearms and forced me into a sitting position. She put her hand under my chin and lifted my face to look at her. "Mommy," she said, "do you know how much more it would hurt Michael if you stopped doing what you love to do?"

I took into my heart what she was saying to me.

She continued. "He would never want us to stop living, even if he couldn't go on. You can't quit. You have to show everyone that we have faith."

I wrapped my arms around my daughter. Here she was, cut to the core by losing her brother and best friend, yet somehow she knew exactly what to say to sustain me. And I knew it was what Michael would say to me, too.

She was my rock that night and every night for a while until I could find solid ground for myself.

Still, not a day goes by that he isn't my first thought in the morning and my last thought before I fall asleep. I hear his cute chortle when we go for a family night to a funny movie. I see his eyes light up when we try a new restaurant and the menu is full of delectable choices. I felt him near my shoulder when I married the love of my life, Steve, again. And we chose to get married on May 4, the birth dates of both Michael and my mother. He is the gentle hand on the back of my younger children, steering them safely to school and back home each day. I hear in the voices of my older children how he has changed their lives, as they make new decisions, set new priorities, and honor the blessings of their individual gifts. And on days when I think it's too much, I see his forehead scrunched up in "the Face," and I laugh, because he would want me to. I know that he's still with me and that I will see him again.

But it doesn't ever get better. I've come to accept that.

These words are on the page, not for me, but for you. Look at those you love. There may be a Mallard in your family or among your friends. You have to look closely because they are often the ones who seek no attention at all. On the water, mallards look so serene. They appear to glide effortlessly. Yet right under the surface, their feet push the water, twisting and turning, steering them over the waves that might drag them under. They have to paddle continuously just to stay afloat. Give them a safe nest. Please, don't wait. Remember, depression doesn't wait until Monday.

Grace

Openness to the bounties of life, trusting that we are held in God's love through all circumstances.

*In Los Angeles, Mike's
first week of college.
With his extremely
proud mother, 2009.*

STEVE CRAIG

THE EYE-ROLLING EFFECT

My youngest, Abigail, loves to sing. The day of her first-grade presentation, "Stone Soup," where she was the featured singer, 2009.

$\mathcal{M}$y first grader had followed me out to my car as I was leaving for work. It was January, one of those 40 degree evenings in Las Vegas when the wind whipping down from the barren hills surrounding the city forces me to wonder why any pioneer ever thought to settle this land. It's a thought I know I will have again when it's July and the winds are 118 degrees of gusting hot air. And I'm not talking about Donny.

I'm talking about blazing summer heat. I've had soaking-wet pool towels dry to a crisp so quickly that they look more like some freaky terry cloth sculpture that can stand up on its own. It's a small price to pay, those two or three uncomfortable months, because the rest of the months of the year in Las Vegas are desert bliss.

I quickly hugged my daughter good-bye and encouraged her to hurry back into the house because she was barefoot and without a jacket. When I got into the car I noticed that she was still dawdling near the front walk, trying to pick up small decorative garden stones with her toes. To most adults, it probably seems like everything distracts a six-year-old from the request at hand. But after going through seven six-year-olds before Abigail, I had figured out that they aren't distracted; it's more that everything in their world can be turned into a daring challenge to be conquered. My challenge was to get her out of the cold. Her challenge was to grasp pebbles with her toes and lift them as high as her leg would allow before they fell.

I have to admit, I wasn't so sure that her challenge was really a worthless "distraction." After all, "grasping with the toes" is a skill I've used myself many times. I've slipped off a shoe to grab tubes of mascara that have fallen under the dressing room table, recover pens that rolled under desks, and even napkins that slipped off my lap at a restaurant. I've got some arthritis in my neck, but, hey, my toes are pretty limber!

Halfway down the driveway, I stepped on the brake and rolled down the window. "Abigail Olive May! Please get in the house right now! It's too cold out here for you."

Abi looked up at me with a bit of a frown and then took a deep breath in and closed her eyes for a moment.

Oh, no, I thought to myself. She's way too young to start in on delivering a deep, exasperated sigh capped off with an eye roll. My other kids had been at least eleven before that preteen trait kicked in.

Thankfully, this time she proved me right. After taking a deep breath, she thrust her foot one more time into the pebbles along the path and squeezed her toes, picking up a rounded stone.

"Mommy! Watch this!"

With her sturdy little "Fred Flintstone" foot, she flung the stone about two feet down the sidewalk. She looked up at me, her hand raised in the air, as if she had just qualified for the Olympics.

These are the times when having to go to work is so difficult. There are such a limited number of years when a child is exhilarated by unself-conscious discovery of the world at large. As a working mom, I feel like I've missed so many of those fun or silly moments with all of my children. Not that "toe grasping" is a rite of passage that should get any special attention, but it's wonderful to be a part of those years in a child's life when everything is a game to be played. Those years pass by so quickly, soon giving way to the double-digit age when everything I ask them to do is an "imposition" on their free will. I can tell that they think that I am being ridiculous in almost all of my requests even though they never say it out loud.

Disrespectful back talk was never allowed in my parents' home when I was growing up, and even though I want to hear what my children are thinking, it's not allowed in my home either. I'm willing to discuss almost anything with my children, as long as the discussions are civilized. Learning how to have a discussion is a really important life skill . . . maybe a bit greater than "toe grasping"! Still, it doesn't stop kids from saying "volumes" through their nonverbal cues.

I'm now on midteenagers number five and six and early teenager number seven, so I can recognize these unspoken signals better than a member of the Audubon Society can recognize a blue-tip hummingbird in flight.

As an amateur student of quantum physics, I love to read any article on cause and effect, perhaps because my daily life with eight kids is a metaphor for the chaos theory. You may have heard of "the Butterfly Effect," which proposes the scenario that a butterfly flapping its wings in Brazil can become the impetus for a tornado in Texas. I can do my own personal home study on that effect. I can feel the ripple effect of a child sighing and rolling his eyes in the upstairs corner of his bedroom two floors down to where I am at the kitchen counter. It usually follows one of my *way*-over-the-top requests like "Isn't it your turn to feed the dog?" or "You're the one who left your permission slip in the car. Go get it and then I'll sign it." The storm of frustration slowly begins its swirl, released by the sigh and the eye rolling. I've come to the conclusion that it must be a natural physiological response in the adolescent body. A deep sigh causes the muscles around the eyes to relax, rolling them toward the top of the head. This releases the frustration and prepares the adolescent (the same child who can walk a shopping mall from end to end on a Saturday afternoon) for the insurmountable task of walking the short hallway to the garage to get his or her own permission slip.

I know I'm not the lone mother who has to ignore this phase of adolescence as best as I can. We moms need an AA group: Adolescent Aggravation. I won't chase the storm my kids brew no matter how much they "flap" about what I ask them to do, because there is a part of me that completely remembers feeling the exact same way, way back when.

I have my own vivid recollections of feeling the same when

I was a young teen. There were many times when my mother's demands on my personal time made me exclaim silently in my head, "Are you kidding me?"

My mom knew that the best way to remind me that show business doesn't make a person exempt from everyday life was to have me join her in the regular household chores when I got home from the recording studio or the TV studio.

I would walk through the front door, exhausted from a ten-hour day in the studio, to have her greet me at the door with a basket of fresh cherries or a set of measuring cups in hand and a grin on her face. I knew that the next two hours would be time with my mother learning to bottle fresh fruit or baking homemade bread. There was no escaping it. As a teenager, I thought it was the pits, figuratively. My mother knew that coring out the cherry pits (literally) or filling my hands with sticky dough was a great way to take my mind off the materialistic "dough" and put it back on what matters most: family. I'm certain I rolled my eyes and sighed about her requests, too. She didn't seem to mind, as long as we rolled out the bread together and talked. It was in those hours that I discussed my problems and fears with her, and she listened deeply. My mom was crafty that way.

I was a very strong-willed girl, though, and if I thought I had a justifiable point of view, I would rarely back down until I was heard.

One afternoon, my mother and I were in the kitchen making dinner, discussing what dress I would be allowed to wear to a big event. Both of my parents had a firm standard of modesty, which is a principle of my faith, as well. However, it often seemed that my mother's idea of what was appropriate for a girl my age was nothing short of a pilgrim-style dress from the 1600s. That's an exaggeration, of course—she was fine with anything that came up to my chin and down to my calves! My idea for the dress for the event fell more in the 1970s current-trend category. Come on! Halter tops ruled.

My mother was listening to me, but she didn't seem to be changing her mind about my wardrobe choice. She kept shaking her head no even when I brought up what I thought were convincing points that seemed logical to me. She just continued peeling the carrots and tried to change the subject to something else.

I could tell I was losing ground. Losing to a mother who was wearing a purple muumuu.

For a brief number of years, muumuus were my mother's way to dress when she was home. She loved bright colors and big flowers and lots of room to move around in. The muumuu fit all of those requirements. To keep her hair out of the way when she was busy, she would sweep it up into a tall pile on top of her head. The big lenses of her glasses always seemed to have something smudged on them from cooking or gardening or putting makeup on in a hurry.

My teenage self realized, "Of course, she'll never see my point of view. She doesn't care about fashion." But I tried one more time.

"Mother, I'm grown up now, in case you hadn't noticed. I can't wear a dress that makes me look like a baby."

She said nothing back. I'm sure at this point I sighed and rolled my eyes.

I couldn't believe she was being so stubborn.

I stood staring at my mother and thought, "I could take you down."

Instantaneously, I realized that my mouth was moving with my thought and I had actually said it out loud. What was I thinking???? A bit of panic set in, but I had no choice but to hold my stance.

My mother set down her vegetable peeler and swiveled her head to look me in the eyes. "You think so?"

The next thing I knew, I was looking up at the ceiling. My mother had dropped me gently to the linoleum in a swift martial-arts-type move that I never saw coming.

More astounding was that she had pinned all 103 pounds of me by laying her body across the top of mine. I wasn't at all hurt, but I was in shock.

My mother then burst into laughter.

It wasn't a cruel laugh, just a silly one, brought on by the look of surprise on my face.

I had to laugh, too. Who knew that my mother was hiding some muscle under that muumuu? She had superpowers that I had never suspected. I was stunned and speechless. The Purple Muumuu Master had taken me down!

Needless to say, I wore the dress that my mother wanted me to wear, and despite all my earlier protests, I didn't look "like a baby," but I didn't look like a sexy woman, either. I looked like a young teenager, which is what I was. I only had to wear that dress for one night, but the awe and admiration I felt for my mother's ability to lovingly answer my challenge lasted from that day forward. A mother can't convey to her child the wisdom the years have given her, but she can stand firm in her no, because the no comes from knowing what is best for her child.

There are around twenty-eight hundred different species of butterflies around the world. Each group probably has millions of members, all flapping their wings. If "the Butterfly Effect" is real, there must be new storms starting up every second. I'm sure, for the sake of education, at least one butterfly of every known species has been pinned to a board. It only takes one example: One storm-inciting butterfly must fall for us to be able to see the bigger picture.

The wind was gusting through my open car window as my little Abi's face popped up next to the door handle.

"Mommy, can I go to the show with you tonight?" she pleaded. "Please! It's Friday. No school tomorrow."

She loves to be at the show with me, to have me all to herself for one whole hour to tell me the many adventure stories from her life as I put on makeup and curl my hair.

I didn't stand firm. "Okay," I said. "You need your boots and a jacket and bring a coloring book and some markers."

Abi's face beamed.

"Hurry. Run like the wind. Mommy is late."

I love having her go to the show with me, too, even though thirty minutes before the end of the show she's usually sound asleep on the couch in my dressing room. I wanted to enjoy every moment of this time in Abigail's life when no one's opinion or attention matters more to her than mine. Let it last, I prayed silently. Let it last.

Temperance

Self-control in words and actions.

MARCIA WILKIE

One positive aspect of working evenings is being able to attend my kids' daytime school events. With Abigail and Matthew, 2009.

HOE TO THE END OF THE ROW

My working performer family, waiting for yet another bus ride to another show: (from left) Donny, Wayne, Father, Jay, Alan, Mother, me, and Jimmy. Donny, Jimmy, and I were already singing songs in Swedish and Japanese.

*M*y father's bassinet was a wooden fruit box stored under a tree at the edge of the wheat field. Tethered to the same tree with a long piece of soft clothesline rope tied around their waists were my dad's older brothers, who at ages two and five might have wandered away. The oldest brother was in charge of watching the two younger ones. The big shady tree was their babysitter from dawn until the noon hour. The only lullaby that was heard was the swishing noise the machetes made cutting the stalks close to the ground to harvest the crop. One of the workers in the field, and the only female, was Grandmother Osmond as a young woman, age twenty-three. This was the way she provided for her three young sons.

My grandmother didn't have the choice to be a stay-at-home mom. Grandfather Osmond, who my brother Donny has always resembled, had been killed by a bucking horse. The blow from the horse's hoof ruptured my grandfather's spleen, causing immediate and severe internal bleeding. He died within an hour in my grandmother's arms. My father was only six weeks old when this happened. There were no EMTs for my grandmother to call, no extra money set aside, no life insurance policy, and no government services that she could turn to for assistance. She couldn't lean on family and friends as it was the middle of World War I and most of their relatives were also struggling to get by. There weren't many opportunities for a young widow with children, so she relocated her little family often to find work: from Wyoming to Idaho to Utah to California and then back to Wyoming until finally ending up in Ogden, Utah.

I'm pretty sure that my father didn't have many memories of carefree days without some type of hard labor that was necessary just to get by. As he grew up, no one ever asked him if he "felt like" working. Even as a child, he had to pull his weight and contribute to the family as soon as he could. By the time my father was five, my grandmother had married a man who wanted a wife. Not sure he was at all interested in the thought of raising children, though. She wasn't wholeheartedly enamored of him, but he provided some relief for her in a world where being a single mom was frowned upon. He was a talented piano player and saw great opportunity in my young father, who had a powerful singing voice for a small boy. He would sit my dad on top of an upright piano and have him belt out popular tunes of the day. Then he would have my dad pass the hat for coins.

My father knew what was expected of him and complaining was never an option; this man was a tough character with very little patience. Whenever the stepfather was displeased with my father for any reason, he was left outside to sleep under the porch steps, which happened more times than my father could count. My dad's two older brothers were pressured to be out on their own at very young ages. As soon as Dad was old enough to lift and carry a heavy bag, he delivered and sold newspapers; by age fifteen, after an altercation in which he had to physically defend his mother from his stepdad, he was kicked out of the house and left to survive alone, responsible for putting the clothing on his back and figuring out how to get an education.

My brother Merrill recently met a man at a retirement home who had known my father back then. He told a story my father had never shared with us. After being homeless for a bit and sleeping near a river, my father made his way to a cousin's home in Idaho and instantly went out to try to find work. The man described how my father had come to the store owned by his family to ask for a job. He was turned down, but he didn't let that discourage him. He returned the next day with a broom and began cleaning the doorway and sidewalks in front of the store. The day after that, he held the door open for customers and greeted them. The customers took note and commented on the courteous boy at the door. By the end of the week, he was hired to work inside the store, where he started out sweeping floors and quickly took on more and more responsibility. The owner ended up liking my father's work ethic to such a degree that he hired him to help out at his house, too. This man at the retirement home told my brother that he remembers how my father would sing while he worked and always had a cheerful attitude, even when doing very hard labor. For example, at one point he was given just one week to dig a half-mile ditch that was three feet deep, all on his own.

Before I was born, my father had worked many, many types of jobs, often two full-time jobs: raising chickens, taxi driver, box factory carpenter, shoe salesman, railroad brakeman, radio ad salesman, real estate broker, cattleman, door-to-door salesman, and then finally an entertainment businessman.

During his army service in England during World War II, he was a sergeant responsible for the construction of aircraft runways. For a time, he was stationed in a shipyard that was close to being bombed out on numerous occasions. My father was a witness to mass destruction and death and returned home with what we now call PTSD—post-traumatic stress disorder. There was no diagnosis or support for the aftereffects of wartime traumas at that time. He had to find his own way of dealing with the memories and repercussions of his years of service. On top of being on "the move" throughout his entire childhood, the stress disorder made it hard for my father to feel settled and safe anywhere. It seemed that he was always aware of potential dangers that might harm his loved ones. Like me, he was always the most at peace when he had all of his children nearby.

The most noticeable long-term effect of all of his early-life responsibility was that my dad was uncomfortable with any unstructured leisure time. In my mother's journals of 1998, the year my father turned eighty-two, almost every entry contains a mention of the work that filled my father's day: *"pulled the weeds," "planted tomatoes," "cleaned out the basement," "fixed the VCR," "painted the hallway,"* and on and on.

When my brothers and I were still children, my father's "fun" days consisted of teaching us to round up the cattle, weed and plow a garden, repair the dock on the pond, paint the house, or mend barbed wire fences. My parents often used the age-old saying "An idle mind is the devil's workshop." Both of them made sure that our minds weren't left to "idle" for very long. We were encouraged to pursue our interests as individuals, but almost always under the watchful eyes of at least one of my parents.

For my father, sitting on a porch and just watching the world go by rarely happened until he was in his late eighties and only because someone would insist that he slow down. The most inactive he would ever be is when he would sit in a boat or lakeside to fish for an hour or two. The silver lining of my father's tough childhood was that he developed a skill that he passed on to me and my brothers: being self-reliant through understanding our resources and through lots of hard work. Thank you, Dad—and I mean it!!

I made my first paycheck at age three, singing on the *Andy Williams Show* with my brothers. That was about the same age I started doing the "unpaid" chores that were expected of us at home. In our house, if you were tall enough to reach the table, then you could set the table or clear the dishes. If you were old enough to catch a fish, then you were big enough to learn to clean it and prepare it for dinner. If you could toast and butter your bread, then you could also make it and bake it. The fresh vegetables we had with dinner were the ones that we had planted, weeded, and harvested in the garden with our hands.

No task was ever done halfway. Every single one of my brothers would tell you that my father's motto for life was the gardening-themed "Hoe to the end of the row," or as we would probably say today, "If it's worth doing, it's worth doing well." To my dad, "good enough" didn't equal "well," and that also applied to our performances. A song didn't belong onstage until it could be performed well: the harmonies, the choreography, and each musical instrument coordinated in perfect order.

Dad's idea of "to the end of row" also meant that after the show, you took care of your own costumes, packed up your own gear and instruments, and helped to load the tour bus to the next destination. On many days the rehearsal process seemed endless, and there were very few spare hours to ride a bike or play ball. All nine of us worked really hard to do shows. My mother worried about it and would have sleepless nights over how *hard my kids work.* She wrote of this in her journals quite often. Yet she was also the role model for the word "effort." She had fifty projects going on any given day and almost never sat down for more than fifteen minutes to eat a meal. I have very few childhood memories of seeing my mother sleep. Even when we toured in a shared Airstream trailer or tour bus, she would be working away when I went to bed and working away when I got up the next morning. And I slept very little!

When my career was first getting national attention, following the release of "Paper Roses" in 1973, the feminist movement in the U.S. was in full gear on the street, in office buildings, on the sports fields, in the schools, and in the halls of government and other institutions. The movement wanted the world to know that women could handle any job a man could do and deserved equal pay for it, too. Their accomplishments changed the face of everyday life forever, but it was a life I was blessed to have already. By age fifteen, I had equal billing and equal pay with my brother on a hit television variety show on which I had set a new record of being the youngest female to ever host a national TV show. At a time when millions of women were renouncing their lives as homemakers to join the workforce, I had no idea what it was like to spend much time at home. My sense of home was wherever my mother and father were, which as an entertainment family often meant temporary living arrangements. Just as countless women longed to be identified by a job title, the one thing I knew I could already do was work. In fact, as a teenager approaching adulthood, I was beginning to crave what these millions of women were moving down their personal priority list: home, husband, children.

When I first became a single mom, I toured all the country music venues I could, up to three hundred days a year, to support my son Stephen and myself. Stephen took to singing very early on and was a natural performer at age three and a half. By age four, he would don a cowboy hat, boots, and a big silver belt buckle and go onstage to sing "All My Exes Live in Texas" with my band. It would bring the house down every time, and it gave me about four minutes to do a quick costume change. One evening he made a mistake, forgetting the words. He dropped the microphone and ran offstage crying. In my distress over the stage being left empty during a show, I remember scolding him: "Never cry onstage. If you make a mistake, pick it back up and finish the song." He wiped his tears with the sleeve of his cowboy shirt as I continued channeling my father's words: "I'm going to be so disappointed in you if you don't finish your song."

My little son took a deep breath, put his hat back on, and went back out onstage. He not only finished—he nailed the song and got a standing ovation. But suddenly that didn't matter to me anymore. I felt sick to my stomach that I had talked to him that way. I had applied my dad's motto of "Hoe to the end of the row," the same principle he applied to every aspect of our careers, but it didn't feel right. I understand my dad's perspective, because in television at that time, most of the shows were shot before a live audience. You couldn't do three or four takes. You had one chance, and that meant no mistakes. There were no contracts, and you were invited back only if the audience liked you, one appearance at a time. To this day, crew people who have worked in Hollywood for forty years say to me, "We've still never worked with a group as professional as you guys were, even as kids. We called you the 'One-Take Osmonds.'"

My father was our driving force. He did make us work hard. I know we wouldn't have the career portfolios we have today if my father hadn't applied his work principles to us. But it didn't make for a carefree childhood, and that was what made me feel so upset after I scolded Stephen. He was only a small boy. I knew from personal experience the pressure he must have been feeling. I had to ask myself: Why was I making him feel like he was there to work? It was this experience that changed my outlook on how I would raise my own children.

When I remarried and my family started growing, I couldn't stand the thought of my kids working as hard as I had during my childhood. I hoped to give them more of a stress-free childhood than I had had and allow them to really be kids. Their chores were very minimal, and if I sensed that something felt like too much pressure or stress to them, I would give them support to get through it. They had fun birthday parties, Disney videos, popular toys and bikes, and long summer and holiday vacations without any responsibilities. At least, that's what I thought at the time.

Because I worked so hard as the family provider, whenever I had Mommy time with my kids, I made up for my sense of guilt by using my credit card. That usually meant an excursion to get the newest video games on the shelf, the hottest trends in clothes and shoes, the "had to see and have" movies, toys, and treats. In reality, I probably gave each kid more money to spend on games at Chuck E. Cheese in one evening than my parents spent on all of their kids' birthday presents. Most of the time, my kids wouldn't even have to ask me for things. I would offer it all to them, hoping it made up for the hours and days I had to spend away from them to work. If I had to be away from home for more than a week, I took my children with me if I possibly could, and I almost always took one of the kids along if it was an overnight event. It gave me special one-on-one time with each child. I loved having these overnights with each child individually, but I would try to make it an even happier time by stopping in at the local mall. Shopping became an activity we did together. It was easy, and it was available no matter where my work took me. And it seemed to always make my child happy, at least for that day. In retrospect, it was something that made only me happy. My children have very few memories of shopping excursions and the gifts they were given. What they remember most are the bonding experiences: the sights we saw and the stories that could be told about the adventures we had together. None of those stories ever started with, "That was the time Mom bought me a . . ."

While I was growing up, shopping was a favorite and safe activity for my mother and me, especially when the family was on tour. But our shopping was never a "spree" and was always preceded by long days of concerts or commercial shoots. My mother would take me to pick out just one special doll or outfit as a reward for the long working days I endured as a child. There's a big difference between a child working to earn a reward and a child who feels deserving of anything he wants because he knows his parents have the money to get it for him.

In her journal of 1974, while we were on tour in Osaka, Japan, my mother wrote:

"Marie and I went shopping with Kioko. We walked our legs off in a big Fantasy underground shopping mall. Three bodyguards for Marie went along with us. I bought slippers for George and a plastic cape for rain. Marie bought a sweater set and a scarf.

"We weren't able to buy much because we already spent our limit!"

My parents gave us spending limits until we were eighteen years old. Even when *Donny & Marie* was the number one show on ABC and I was the highest-paid child on television, I was given an allowance of three hundred dollars per month, but not until I turned seventeen years old. In 1977, that was a lot of money for a teenager. But it was expected that I would use it to buy any clothes or accessories that I wanted for myself. Before the *Donny & Marie* show, there was no allowance given out, at least not in currency. The only allowance we knew was what was expected of us: no allowance for laziness.

When people ask me how I survived being a child celebrity without the self-destruction that seemed to be the curse of many of my peers, I tell them that it was because my parents took their stewardship of their children very seriously. We lived by their rules, not our wishes. More than that, as kids, we never really had enough money to get into any kind of trouble. Once our spending limit was used up, we had to wait until the next month. It made me appreciate the value of everything. I remember being on an international tour, sometimes doing up to three shows in one day, and resisting any temptation to spend a dime until we performed in Paris, France. My dream was to buy clothes by a French designer. My mother wrote in her journal in May 1975: "*I went with Marie to do a little shopping yesterday. She has been waiting patiently to shop in Paris, and wasn't disappointed. The cut of the clothes here seems to be just right for her so she got two outfits. And is she ever happy. She was up late last night trying them on and packing them just so.*"

I can recall almost every detail of those outfits. I've always had designer taste, and Paris was fashion heaven to me. I also remember the feeling of pride that came with knowing I had bought them with money I had budgeted and saved. I appreciated what I got.

On another trip, my dad bought me a gorgeous gold beaded necklace on the Champs-Élysées to celebrate and commemorate my first single, "Paper Roses," when it went gold in numbers of records sold. My mom gave me a pair of her gold-plated earrings to go with it. They meant so much to me as a girl, and still do. I have them framed and displayed in my dressing room. It reminds me that work and effort is the "gold" of feeling self-worth.

Looking back, I regret not giving my older children that experience of appreciation that can only come through working to attain something you want. They might not have just expected that they should (and would) have what they wanted. I had robbed them of one of the most satisfying "rites of passage" that a young person can experience because of my own guilt at having to be away from them for work so often. I wanted them to have fun childhood memories that weren't connected to having to work. Instead, I gave them a false sense of entitlement, which each of them has worked hard to overcome as young adults. I'm so proud of their accomplishments now, despite my early flaws. I know I wasn't alone in allowing children to expect rewards. I believe our society is accelerating the speed of the runaway train of instant gratification. Recently I was at a child's birthday party when the mother I was standing next to questioned whether our kids should really get a "goodie bag" chock-full of toys at another child's birthday party. She had a point. Wasn't the idea of a birthday party to celebrate a friend and to "give" to them without receiving? I don't think my kids need a certificate of accomplishment for completing every project they do, especially when it took only two or three hours of their time. Another friend of mine with young children pointed out to me at a recent soccer tournament where every single team got a trophy, "Not every team wins in soccer; so giving every child a trophy seems to take away their drive to improve."

The other day I heard my ten-year-old say, "It's taking forever to download this video." I'm hoping that we haven't all gone too far down this track of impatience and entitlement. My daughter looked at me in the wide-eyed horror of deprivation when I pulled the plug on the computer and announced that it was "being put away for the weekend." I wish I had a garden I could have sent her out to weed!

I still occasionally take one of the younger four children with me on my overnight events, when it doesn't interfere with schoolwork, but the credit card rarely comes out of my wallet. Now the time is spent in one-to-one talks over flavored ICEEs and burgers about life, social issues, hopes, and dreams. If they want to buy something, the younger children know that at least half of the money has to be earned beforehand. Both Brandon and Brianna went on school trips to Europe over spring break in 2012. I wanted them to go because I believe it's so important for teenagers to see how other societies live and have preserved their heritage for many years before America was even discovered. It also helps them understand world history and the freedoms we enjoy here. It was an opportunity the older four children had while touring with me, but the younger four had very little travel experience. However, I knew that I couldn't just give Brandon and Brianna the trips and have them fully appreciate the experience. Both of them had to work, doing extra and more extensive chores around the house: babysitting, cleaning out the garage and the pantry, sorting through outgrown clothing, and scrubbing out the fountain in the backyard. By the time they got on the plane, they had each earned their spending money and paid for half the trip. My thirteen-year-old, Matt, is now working toward his school trip for next year.

Brandon is the last kid old enough to remember the "glory days" of Mom's shopping extravaganzas. One day when he was fourteen he said, "I wish I had been born as one of the older kids. They had it good! They didn't even have to work for it." He's right. Materially, they had it good, but it didn't ease my guilt and it also gave them a wrong message: that a mother's love means you get gifts and toys. Now they've paid the price and know the joys of hard work and frugality. My younger kids enjoy the time we spend together doing simple things when I can give them my undivided attention.

With my first four children, it was more than gifts and toys that gave them the wrong message. They went on the road with me to every country music fair, festival, and honky-tonk and also toured for months with me on my international tours of *The King and I* and *The Sound of Music*.

At eleven, Stephen auditioned for the part of Kurt in *The Sound of Music* and was cast in my national tour. He didn't get the part because he was my son but because he earned the role. He went on to do exceptionally well for the two years that we performed together. All four children would join me for a number or two onstage for my holiday touring show, *The Magic of Christmas*. They had a great education in different cultures, geography, and adapting to new environments. They got an up-close perspective on how Americans appear to people in different countries. However, keeping late show business hours, having room service meals and laundry service, leaving every hotel bed unmade, and being driven wherever we needed to go gave them a false sense of reality. They became very adept at chatting with adults, from theater investors to the music director to restaurant staff and hotel bellhops, but missed out and had to play catch-up on the concept of how effort leads to reward and how follow-through in day-to-day activities keeps it all going forward.

It was never a matter of laziness. They are each very motivated in their various career paths. They learned to play musical instruments, edit music, sew, play sports, bake, paint, draw, dance, and do scouting and photography. I think the passion of the artistic associates in my life influenced them greatly. They learned a lot about applying themselves to learn a skill, no matter how difficult.

As a young mother, I chose to allow my kids to have time to discover for themselves what they were interested in, what their gifts were, and then to encourage them to devote themselves to it wholeheartedly. However, what I know now is that children discover their capabilities through effort and gaining an understanding of what it means to live in and contribute first to a family and then to a community. You should sort out life and sort laundry at the same time. As I said on Oprah a few years ago, you can't buy self-esteem for your child. It has to be developed individually.

When the younger four children came along, the older four had to take on more responsibility. It was a tough learning curve at first, because they didn't "see" what needed to be done. They just expected it all to be done by someone else. However, soon enough they realized that work went into having a home, not just a house, and helping to raise their younger siblings. They would help with baths and feedings, cleaning out the car, laundry, baking, and household chores. As the younger four got older, they would drive them to sports and scouts, dance classes and church events. Even now, they will stop by to help with homework, stay overnight if I have to be away, and take the kids to the movies or out for fun. It has made us a real tight family.

One of my girlfriends told me that her twenty-two-year-old nephew called her the month after he graduated from college and said that he was "in trouble." When my friend asked what was wrong, he answered, "I don't know how to do real life."

My friend thought it was humorous for a minute until she realized that his concern was real and serious. He explained, "You know my parents wanted me to not stress over anything in high school and college so that I could study and get good grades. And that's what I did. But now I'm sharing an apartment with friends who laugh at me because I've never done laundry and I don't know how. I've never had to change the sheets on a bed or take my car for an oil change. I just made my first grilled cheese sandwich last week. Even more humiliating, I'm applying for jobs with a college degree, and I don't have a résumé that shows that I ever earned a dime in my life. What should I tell them?"

Even though I'm a mother, it took me a long time to appreciate that putting forth effort to be a contributing member of a family and a community is crucial to growing into a well-adjusted and functioning adult who can make a living and build a life of your own. Isn't that what all parents hope for their child? Now when my kids complain about chores, I tell them that my job as a mother is to make certain that they can stand on their own two feet and know how to take care of themselves and their homes.

Children need—literally—to learn to stand, and walk, on their own. No conscientious mother would grab up one-year-old every time she attempts to balance on two feet and carry her where she wants to go. The baby has to learn to control her own muscles through trial and error. We know that it's impossible to carry our kids through life physically after a certain age, but it seems like many current-day mothers hesitate to let children learn to find their life paths through trial and error. We might accept that a toddler can just point to what they want, but by age three, our hope is that our children can use speech to communicate and walk or even run to what they want. To take that effort away from children is to stall their natural development.

Most of my own kids, as toddlers, wanted to "help." When I was a two-year-old, my mother kept a bottom drawer full of cleaning rags in the kitchen. I couldn't wait for there to be a spill so I could enthusiastically get out a towel to clean it up, just to be a help to my mom. My own children wanted to "work" alongside me on almost any household chore. They would stand on a chair next to me if I made dinner and add in the "greedy ants," as my youngest called ingredients. They would actually demand to push the vacuum and "test" the suction by dropping dry Cheerios on the rug. When Abigail was three, her biggest smile of the day was when she had a glass cleaner spray bottle and two paper towels in hand. Both of our sliding glass doors would get a good cleaning. Well, at least from the floor to two and a half feet up the door, as high as she could reach. I know it must be pretty common for little children to want to feel useful because millions of toy stoves and ovens, little shopping carts, tiny lawn mowers, and play garden tools are sold every year. They want to emulate us. So why do we deprive them of their definition of usefulness when we can help them with their self-worth by always appreciating and praising their good efforts?

My younger four children now have their assigned chores, which they know are their responsibility. They each have to keep their own rooms picked up and wash and put away their own clothes. Then they take turns taking out the garbage, loading the dishwasher, feeding and walking the dog, sweeping the kitchen floor, cleaning out the inside of the car, carrying in the groceries, loading the washing machine and the dryer, picking up the yard area, and keeping their homework area organized. When they complain, I tell them that I'm making them strong so they can fly.

One of the best metaphorical stories I've heard about effort is one I tell my children often, for their sake and also to remind myself of its message. It's a good one to demonstrate that our best intentions to help might hurt in the long run.

The story goes this way:

A man is out for a walk in a wooded area on a summer day. He looks closely at a tree branch and finds a cocoon. He sees a butterfly attempting to free itself from the cocoon by chewing a hole to escape. Feeling bad for the tiny butterfly's Herculean efforts, the man pulls the cocoon apart with his fingers and the small butterfly falls free into the palm of his hand.

The man expects the butterfly to spread its wings and claim its freedom, but instead the butterfly tips over sideways, folds his wings and dies, never taking flight once. What the man didn't understand was that he had interrupted the process of struggle, which gives a butterfly the chance to let its wings dry off and gain strength in its jaws to be able to feed itself, increasing its chance of survival.

Now, this story usually works better on young children than on teenagers. When I tried to repeat the story to my thirteen-year-old daughter, she sighed and said, "I know, Mother. But I don't think I'm going to die if someone else loads the dishwasher tonight."

Yes, I had to work very hard as a young girl, but like most children, my kids don't want to hear about it. What I try to share with them is that by the time I was sixteen, I had gained some important insights, starting with a deep understanding of how to work in the service of others. Every occupation or even every idea has to be something that will serve other people in some way.

I saw an interesting interview in the *New York Times* with Amy Astley, editor for *Teen Vogue* magazine. Asked about her hiring practices, she said, "I'll see someone who was a waitress for many summers and I'll say, 'Well, tell me about that.' In today's upwardly mobile résumé, you don't always see that. You often see kids who've never had a job. But I love seeing someone who scooped ice cream or was a waitress. To me, it means they had to make some money and they had a job dealing with the public. . . . I had jobs like that, too, when I was a kid. I respect it. I respect all forms of work, and I don't see it on a lot of résumés anymore."

When it comes to a work ethic, I find it interesting that all of the people who work closest to me in my company—my most trusted allies—are people who had to work as teenagers. And most of them earned money before they could legally be employed. I can count on each of these people to put at least 110 percent into any project I hand them. I've also observed that they each have a high level of common sense, frugality with resources, and the ability to "see the forest for the trees."

A college degree is always a very worthwhile goal, but it doesn't count for much unless a personal work ethic comes with it. I think more employers are realizing that job experience for teenagers makes them more eligible for handling a real job and all of the issues that come with it. After all, it's not up to employers or teachers or therapists to teach our children the value of a good work ethic. It's up to us as parents.

Kids learn through watching. An old proverb goes "If you give a man a fish, he is hungry again in an hour; if you teach him to catch a fish, you feed him for a lifetime." My daughter Rachael works with me as a wardrobe assistant and designer for my Las Vegas show and assists me on my TV talk show. She puts in twelve-hour days right along with me. One day she told me, "Mom, the one thing I always like about myself, even when I have bad days, is that I know how to work hard. I learned that from you. You gave me the ability to count on myself and to know that I can figure out solutions and provide for myself. I love you for that."

I learned the same values by watching my parents' work ethic in action and the expectations that they had for each of us to be equally industrious. They taught me that the rewards we seek, both financial and personal, are the result of discipline and accomplishing worthwhile goals. Of course, being a child, I always wanted to push back against the structure. I didn't see the necessity of learning to bake bread after I had worked for fourteen hours taping a TV show. I didn't think that learning to bottle fresh cherries was a good way to spend time, especially when you could get whatever you wanted at a grocery store. Weeding the garden, rounding up cattle, and cleaning toilets seemed like jobs a performer shouldn't have to do. I wanted to look at magazines or tan in the sun or get a facial, which I never did. I appeared in the teen magazines of that time looking pale with a face full of zits! However, being involved in a community or society gave me a great perspective on helping others find happiness, and I saw how putting in extra effort could benefit my whole family. My mother believed and would say: *"Discipline is a muscle. You have to strengthen it to be able to do the things you want to do in this life."*

My parents were very insightful, knowing that if we take away the struggles and effort that are necessary to build self-esteem, then we are, in some way, encouraging the idea that the goal for the next generation is merely to figure out a way to have someone else pay for their needs and wants. It's an attitude we can't afford, especially when you read the statistics that 45 to 50 percent of Americans receive some type of government aid. Making others work harder so that you don't have to is the wrong message to send to our kids. I worry as I see our government support a system that takes away the desire to be self-sufficient by giving people money and benefits that haven't been earned, eventually leading them to feel they deserve it. It takes away from a person's self-respect when they stop earning on their own. It creates entitlement and sometimes laziness and often neglects those who really are in need of help.

My youngest, Abigail, was excited to start kindergarten right after we moved to Las Vegas. About two weeks into the school year, when the honeymoon was over, she exclaimed with exasperation while I was hurrying her into the car for school,

"Oh, I get it now. Every day. Get up. Don't play. Get a bowl of cereal. Get dressed. Get your backpack. Go to school." She leaned back against the seat with a sigh and then said to me, "How many weeks?" I didn't have the heart to tell her "You've only just begun," especially since I was having a hard time keeping a straight face about her jaw-dropping revelation. I gently explained to Abi as I drove that my job was working onstage every night and her job was to learn in school every day. I looked at her little face in the rearview mirror as she absorbed the news of how it was going to be five days a week. Kindergarten really is the beginning of having to show up and be responsible. I encouraged her to learn to love her work like I've learned to love mine. As a mother, I would love to let her be my baby for as long as possible, but that's not the kind of love that will give Abigail self-esteem and happiness as she gets older. It's paid off because now when I suggest that her grades are so good that she's earned a one-day trip away from school with me, she will turn me down, telling me that she has her work to do and I have mine and that we can play on the weekend.

My father was a successful man because he learned the principles of effort and accomplishment from his mother, who knew what it meant to work. I'm sure when she was a young widow living hand to mouth, using a willow tree as a babysitter, and struggling to go where she could find work, she never dreamed that her grandchildren would tour the world, perform for queens and presidents, start national charities, write books, and produce more than 150 gold records. I believe that it was because of my parents teaching us to grow through effort, discipline, and an eagerness to try new things and continue to educate ourselves that my brothers and I have been able to maintain our performing careers for five decades.

In our "get-ahead" society, many stay-at-home moms have been made to feel that they don't have a meaningful job. Please! Who is it, then, that raises the adults who make the decisions, do the research, make technological and medical breakthroughs, provide the necessities of life, and govern the land? Our role as mothers is crucial, especially to the future of our planet. The best way we can contribute is to make sure our kids know how to support themselves and their own families and have decent values in doing it. The principles our children learn at home extend out into our society and eventually the world.

Mothers, fathers, and all parental figures are the role models who daily influence the people who grow up to determine the values of a working society. At the Vancouver Peace Summit in 2009, the Dalai Lama proclaimed to the thousands attending, "The world will be saved by Western women." I think he's right. As mothers, we hold the power to give the world the gift of strong, happy children who can change the course of our future for the better.

Forbearance

Tolerating hardship with good grace. Not allowing the trials of life to steal our joy.

MARCIA WILKIE

Rachael designs all the costumes I wear on-stage and works as my stylist and wardrobe assistant in Vegas, on the road, and on my Hallmark talk show.

WHEN NO ONE IS WATCHING

As always, looking up to both of my parents. On our Huntsville, Utah, property.

Almost everything my parents owned had been spit on. It wasn't because of the nine babies they had raised together and the copious amount of drooling that went on for over twenty years. No. It was *their* spit. The two of them would take aim and spit at the same time. For some reason, it was their personal rite to signify that what they had worked so hard for was finally theirs, fully paid off. They would spit on a new car, the front porch of a new home, a sewing machine, a canoe for the fishing pond, and even new furniture, after the last payment had been put in the mail. (Well . . . they would pretend to spit on the couch. My mother would never truly allow it.) I used to think it was just a goofy quirk of theirs until, as an adult, I happened to read that in ancient Jewish tradition spitting signified legitimate inheritance or ownership, so maybe it was a symbolic gesture passed forward for hundreds of years. It even occurred to me that perhaps this is what started the common and often unconscious motherhood trait of wiping her child's face using her own saliva on a tissue! Not many of us make it to adulthood without one or two swipes of spit from our mothers. When my kids were preschoolers, they would run screaming in the opposite direction if they saw me getting a tissue from my purse.

My parents were both frugal with money, but they were very generous with what they had to share. I don't remember very many Sunday meals where other family members, neighbors, or friends weren't invited to join our dinner table. My mother would make huge meals from whatever the garden had produced that season or, if it was the dead of winter, whatever we had canned and stored in the root cellar. The table would be set with her best rose pattern china. I have a few pieces of her china in my own curio cabinet. When my mother passed away, I gave each of my brothers one place setting to remember our family meals and the importance she gave to that time together. I value that place setting, first, because of the memories, but also because of how much effort and time it took my mother to get every piece. She couldn't buy a complete set on impulse and never asked for it to be given to her as a bride. She would never have even suggested such a costly gift. Instead, my mom collected S&H Green Stamps every time she went to the grocery store. When I was little, she would sit me up on a stool at the kitchen table with an empty stamp book and a stack of sheets of stamps. One or two of my brothers would always want a seat at the table, as well. I would lick each stamp carefully and fill every square and row of the "Quick Saver" book. I actually looked forward to doing this, like it was a game to play. This was before smiley face stickers hit the market! (And long before anyone figured out the peel-

and-stick option.) Once she had collected enough pages of stamps, she would get another place setting of her china pattern. I think it took over three years to get every piece she wanted for her set.

My parents found joy in everything they earned themselves. Early on, when my oldest brothers were still little boys, my dad worked at a real estate business. He would find a little house for sale that was usually in complete disrepair and the two of them would fix it up by hand, with my mother painting, wallpapering, and decorating and my father refurbishing, landscaping, and remodeling. As another brother or two would join the family, my father would sell the little house for a profit and move them all to another fixer-upper that had more room. I can't imagine having to start from scratch over and over, and I'm sure my mother wasn't always anxious to pack everything up again. But my father was always impressed by how adaptable and quick she was. During World War II, when she was only just out of high school, my mother worked for the military in the Utah General Depot as an efficiency expert. The young girl who had helped coordinate getting war materials to where they were needed became the woman who never seemed to be overwhelmed by a home-makeover project while raising five sons. She saw it as a challenge.

My mother was always the one with a grand creative vision, and my father was the facilitator of her plan. Every house became her "dream house." But even when she wrote in her journals about a full day of remodeling the next house project, she always mentions an experience with one of her children, like this one from 1954: *"We scrubbed and cleaned, painted woodwork and papered walls. Soon the place was sparkling clean. We laid a green congoleum rug on the dining room floor and this is one little scene I know I'll always remember when I think of that rug. Wayne* [who was 3] *came in from the kitchen doing a little shuffle step with one foot. We started clapping and praising him for his dance and he said: 'Not many kids can do that.' That statement will surely become a family quote from now on."* My mother's ability to make even chores into a moment of remembered joy made any complaining about hard work seem like needless self-pity.

My mother was never shy about speaking her mind about what would work best for the house and for the family. When I was little, my older brothers would tell me a family story that grew in significance over time. The house had become too crowded, and my visionary mother realized that the vaulted upstairs attic could be turned into an extra room. My father wasn't too enthusiastic about taking on another project in which he would have to put in flooring and windows and also insulate and paint. He tried to dissuade her right before he left for a two-day fishing trip. While he was gone, my mother decided that the only way to accomplish her goal was for my father to have no choice. (I have to admit, I've adopted her clever strategy once or twice in my own adult life.) She went out to the garage and got a sledgehammer and gave the kitchen ceiling a couple of whacks, right where she envisioned the staircase that would lead to the second floor. Let's just say that when my father got back home, he was completely shocked by the gaping hole in the ceiling. Soon he realized it would be just as much work to close the hole in the kitchen ceiling and surrendered to his uncompromising and adorable wife, knowing that she was wise to create more space for their growing family. He took over with a wide smile on his face, completely making over the attic as a playroom and a schoolroom. He painted one wall with blackboard paint and built a chalk tray under it. This is where my mother taught my hearing-impaired brothers to read and speak, and also where my father first taught Alan, Wayne, Merrill, and Jay to sing harmonies.

When my brothers were very young, my mother helped out in a tiny dress shop she co-owned with Grandma Osmond. The best part, she said, was being able to purchase fabrics wholesale. Along with fabric to sew dresses for the customers, she would buy practical shirt material sold by the bolt, which cost significantly less than by the yard. Then she would lay out a shirt pattern, starting with the oldest son and trim it down for the youngest son to make matching shirts for all of my older brothers to wear, at a cost of a little less than a dollar each. She made almost all of my dresses and blouses, adding pleating and crisp cuffs. She had an amazing eye for what colors and designs worked together, something she taught me as a very little girl. Not even a scrap of material would go to waste. Anything left over was turned into a quilt at some point. When I was only five my mother taught me to piece together a small doll quilt from scraps of leftover fabric. It made me feel so accomplished. Ever since then, I've been a lifelong fabric fanatic myself. Quilting is a favorite pastime, one that I'll lose an hour of sleep for if I'm on a roll. Cranston, the fabric company, added me to their list of fabric designers because of my passion for fabric and quilting. They debuted my first fabric collection, called Marie Osmond Heirloom Garden, which I designed. My mother was already quite ill when I had my very first fabric prototypes in hand. I took it all over to her house to show her. Though she had a hard time speaking, her eyes lit up like a child's on Christmas morning. She felt that I had finally "made it," that my fabric collection was the pinnacle accomplishment of my career. I have to say, I was very pleased with the collection myself and have continued to work with Cranston. They have a standard of quality that is hard to top. Even though my mother was never able to physically make another quilt herself, she seemed the most at peace when I would set up a sewing machine near her bed and stitch together rows of a quilt top while I told her all about my day. The sound of a sewing machine running is like comfort food to me, too. I've always felt that everything would eventually be okay when I heard the hum of the machine needle stitching it all together.

There's a saying among quilters that "whoever dies with the most fabric, wins." My mother will always hold the first-place prize! After she had passed away, I took on the monumental task of sorting out her fabric room. And it seriously was a whole room dedicated to fabric, stacks of it, from floor to ceiling.

My daughters helped me, and since they love to sew, they wanted to keep some of the fabrics that they thought were "so sick" and "retro-cool." What made me laugh is that my sweet mother had purchased them in the 1970s, probably on sale, when they actually were cool the first time around. To this day, whenever I design a new doll, quilt, jewelry, or fabric, I always ask myself, "Would my mother like it?"

My father cherished the idea of having almost everything we consumed be homegrown and fresh. He spent most of his life trying to be "green." If he could walk to where he was going instead of using gas, he would do that. He bought a cow to provide milk for the family, and one of my two oldest brothers had the daily chore of milking the cow. My mother pasteurized the milk in a small metal tub, pouring off the cream into mason jars. My dad planted fruit bushes, raspberries and boysenberries, apricot trees, and rows of vegetables. Nothing went to waste, including everything made for every meal, which is how it was growing up with eight brothers. I never even understood the *concept* of leftovers until I was probably ten years old. My mother made her own sun-dried fruits on a screened box my father built. That was our candy. We called them "candy-cots."

Every year for Christmas, each of us would get an orange and a handful of walnuts still in the shell in the bottom of our Christmas stockings, underneath our other small toys and treats. When my parents were children, a simple orange was a delicacy that some people could afford only once a year, especially a widowed mother like Grandma Osmond or two poor schoolteachers like my mother's parents. "Santa" would put them in our stockings to remind us that we were blessed with everything we had.

When "Santa" ate her own orange, she was teaching a lesson in appreciating simple pleasures. She would often comment, "Aren't these oranges delicious? Can you believe we have such good things to eat?" She was always amazed by the bounty of the earth. She would put a raspberry from our backyard into her mouth and say, "Nothing tastes better than homegrown. Isn't it the most joyous creation? What flavor! You can't get that at a grocery store."

Some of the food grown in our garden was shared with neighbors and family, but my mother canned most of it for the winter months. Canning was also a family project. Everyone helped to wash and prepare the fruit, slicing and depitting the peaches and apricots, washing the green beans, boiling and peeling the fresh tomatoes, destemming cherries, and lining up the mason jars and lids. When my mother would open one of her mason jars of canned peaches on a snowy day, you would think she was unwrapping the crown jewels. She'd instruct each of us, "Now don't eat fast. Enjoy them." She and my father would sit at the dinner table, savoring every bite as if they would never taste it again. My brothers and I would grin behind their backs, but the message was clear. We were not to take for granted the bounty of the earth, which was a blessing. My mother even made and bottled her own root beer. It was the best, unless she accidentally put too much yeast in it. Then, sometimes late at night, we would hear the sound of a "pop," like a firework being shot off in the distance. It was one more bottle of root beer exploding in the root cellar.

On Sunday nights, we would watch *The Wonderful World of Disney* and have root beer floats with homemade vanilla ice cream. It's a tradition I've carried forward with my own kids every Sunday: root beer floats and popcorn. Sadly, only the popcorn is homemade in my home and sometimes the ice cream.

Each everyday task, while I was a little girl, was a family affair. Doing the dishes after dinner was a production line with my mother at the sink and each child having a dish towel to dry and put away what they had been handed.

Even when we had all grown up and my parents, in their seventies, moved to a smaller home in Manti, Utah, they still plowed and planted a one-acre garden.

My brother Tom and his family lived next door to them and sometimes I would have to call their house to find out what was going on with my parents, they were so active and busy. I often worried that they were overdoing it. One afternoon, Tom's wife, Carolyn, called me. "You will not believe what your parents are up to now!" she said.

For a minute I was alarmed, until I realized she was laughing so hard she couldn't breathe. "Your father told your mother that he was tired of caring for the oversize garden she had planted and that since there were no kids living at home, they didn't need all the food they were growing. He said he was going to dig it under before the fresh sprouts produced way too much food to handle. She came back with 'Oh, good laws,

George, you just want to go outside and play with your new tractor. Leave it alone.' But your father didn't listen."

It seems my father said, "Say good-bye to the garden, dear. My John Deere and I have work to do." He went outside, hopped on his new tractor, and began digging under the garden at the outer perimeters, making large circles toward the center. Mother ran outside, stood in the center of the garden, and yelled, "You stop it, George!" But he just chuckled and circled closer and closer in. Finally, my mother lay down on the ground, spread-eagle, in front of her rows of peas. As the tractor came near, she screamed and laughed, "Don't you dare take out my last row of peas!!"

My mother won. That fall there was a freezer full of garden peas.

Later in her life, my mother gave me a lot of her canning supplies. Just as my mother taught me, I taught my children to can fruit and bake bread whenever it was possible. I was usually able to get to bottling fruit only once a year, because it was hard to set aside the time.

When she had been sent home from the hospital to live out her life, and about ten months before she died, my mom wrote me a note as I sat next to her bed. It said, "We need to bottle some cherries together soon." I tried to hide my tears that day because I knew that it would probably never happen again, because her physical health was diminishing with every passing week.

Once the Utah Valley cherries were harvested, I decided to make sure her wish came true. With my young daughters, I went to buy several quarts of fresh cherries and took them to Grandma's house, along with all of the canning supplies I had inherited.

The nurse had managed to prop my mother up in a wheelchair so that she could be pushed up to the kitchen table. My girls and I washed and plucked the stems from the cherries and then delivered them to the table, where my mother painstakingly, but with a broad grin on her face, dropped them into the jars, one by one.

The next year, as I was leaving town to go to Philadelphia to do four shows on QVC, my neighbor came over with about ten quarts of fresh-picked cherries from his orchard. My kids love fresh cherries, but I knew that most would probably get soft and be wasted before we could get to them. My mother had passed away months before, and looking at the overflowing box of fruit made my heart ache. I knew that the first thing my mother would have done was get out the canning jars and supplies. I began to cry as I put the cherries on the kitchen counter and left for the airport.

When I got back home three days later, the box of fresh cherries had been replaced by eight jars of cherries. Rachael, though barely a teenager, had remembered the steps her grandmother and I had shown her the previous year and had taken it upon herself to wash and bottle all the cherries. When I complimented her on her self-motivation, she said, "You know, Grandma would have been really unhappy if we had wasted them."

It reminded me that even though children may not appreciate learning something that feels like a chore at the time, they are often glad to have that skill later in life.

A friend of mine who returned to college to study child psychology passed some interesting information on to me a while back. I keep a file of articles and stories that feel life-changing, especially when it comes to parenting. In the journal *Psychology & Marketing* (March 2010), there was a published study showing that most kids—even preschoolers—recognize dozens of corporate logos such as McDonald's, Disney, and sugary breakfast cereals with toys inside. Sadly, there is a growing number of children who have no concept of where food comes from and can't identify certain whole fruits and vegetables. Many children grow up in urban areas where fresh fruits and vegetables are scarce or are weeks old from being trucked across the country. More and more kids never have the experience of growing even simple herbs or seeing an orchard, unlike when we were kids and picking apricots from the trees was an all-day chore. How can children grow to appreciate the blessings of the earth if they have no concept of what the earth produces?

With my parents at the helm, every chore was used as a value lesson about accountability. We were taught to take care of the gifts we had been given: family, talents, health, food, opportunities, our home, and our possessions. We were never allowed to waste anything, unless it was absolutely unavoidable. Most of all, we were held accountable to one another. People always came before possessions.

My father taught me this lesson early in my life. When I was about five, my father came home one evening with little netted bags of foil-covered chocolate coins for each of us. We rarely had "store-bought" candy, and it was considered a big treat if we did. I carried mine around the house, protecting my loot as if it were actual gold coins. Well, it was chocolate, after all. The next day my father asked, "Can I have one of your chocolate coins?"

I couldn't believe he wanted one of mine! He hadn't asked any of my brothers for one of theirs. Why did I have to sacrifice?

Then, in my five-year-old head, I schemed a quick way to keep them all. I told him, "I'm sorry. I would give you one, but I'm saving them all for later." I thought my father would think that I was being wise and frugal and be proud of me, but his face was very disappointed. About twenty minutes later, when I was feeling extremely guilty for my selfishness, I took the chocolate coins to him and said, "Daddy, you can have one." I thought this was the perfect solution. He could have just one, I wouldn't feel guilty anymore, and I could keep the other ten or twelve to myself. I never expected his response in a million years.

"Oh, I don't want one anymore. Since I gave you the whole bag in the first place, I think I'll take the whole bag back." Then he stood up, lifted the bag of candy from my hands, and walked out of the room.

I was devastated, but I knew I couldn't cry over a situation I had created for myself. A bit later, he used the incident as a teaching moment, explaining how God had given us gifts to share, not to hoard and keep to ourselves. He said our blessings were like a pizza that was cut into ten slices. Would you even miss it if you gave one slice to someone else? He likened that to the tithing he paid to the Lord.

About a year later, I used a very liberal interpretation of my father's lesson to justify a moment of kleptomania! This was when my brothers were regulars on the *Andy Williams Show*, and one night we were invited to dinner at the home of a man who did many of the character voices for the Disney cartoons. He and his wife had a daughter who was a few years older than me. We went to play in her room, which was extremely elegant compared to mine at home. She had a gorgeous dresser with a mirror over it and a shelf filled with hundreds of tiny glass animals that captivated my attention. I've always loved the way elephants looked, so I was mesmerized by the little blue glass elephant with his trunk curled up in the air. After a while, the girl went to ask her parents something, and she left me alone in her room. Minutes later, I heard my mother call out that it was time to go home. I thought to myself, "She has a whole shelf full of glass animals. She can share this one with me. She won't even miss it." I cupped the tiny glass elephant in my hand so no one could see it and went out to say my good-byes. I made it all the way to the car, my heart pounding in my chest at the thought of being caught. My teeth were chattering in fear that my parents or hers would figure out that I was a thief. I could see the police car lights and hear the sirens in my imagination.

I took my place in the car, between my parents in the front

seat. It seemed like I had made it! I was going to get away with stealing!

Once the car started up, I knew it was too late to make any other choice, so I kept my hand closed over the little glass animal even tighter. Call it mother's intuition, or maybe I wasn't doing quite the Oscar-winning acting job that I thought I was, but my mother quickly picked up on the fact that I had something to hide. As we drove along, she said, "You're awfully quiet. Is anything wrong?"

"No. Nothing's wrong." I almost choked on my own lie and I could barely swallow.

Once we got home, I was hoping to get the elephant inside and hide it in my room somewhere before anyone knew. My mother got out of the car before me. As I moved to get out of the car from her passenger door, the tiny glass elephant slid out of my hand and shattered on the asphalt. My mother turned at the sound of the shattered glass, which I can't believe she even heard.

"What was that?" she asked.

Since it was dark out, I thought I could still cover my misdeed.

"I don't know," I said, dashing for the front door and leaving the elephant on the driveway.

I can't remember how I was finally pressed to confess, but I vividly recall the shame I felt not only for stealing, but for outright lying to my mother. That shame was worse than any punishment I was given.

The next morning, I went out to pick up the elephant from the driveway, but it was already gone.

Two days later, when the girl's father came to the house to drop something off for my brothers, my mother called me to the front door to tell our good family friend what I had done. I was so embarrassed to confess that I had stolen from his home. I can't even remember his reaction or how it was that I made it up to his daughter. I was overwhelmed by my own humiliation.

A couple of days later, after I had wallowed in my shame and wondered if anyone would ever trust me again, my mother brought out a journal in which she had written down a story her own mother had told her. It was an incident that happened when my grandmother was about five years old. This is how it was written on my mother's journal page:

"I had a little trunk when I was a little girl. We had a cupboard close to the table where we kept our glass dishes. I was cleaning it out one day and discovered a dime on the top of the shelf. I thought it had been there for a long time so I took it and put it in my little trunk. One day my mother said, 'Bill, did you take that dime?' 'No,' he replied. Then she turned to me and said, 'Vera,' and I knew I was doomed. She said, 'Vera, that dime was for a little boy who was running an errand for me.' I confessed I had taken it and bought some penny candy at the post office, then put it in my trunk. I had eaten it all myself because I didn't want anyone to know where I got it. I didn't enjoy the candy, and I didn't enjoy the thought of being a 'thief' either. When I explained to Mother what I had done, she said, 'Vera, don't you ever take anything that doesn't belong to you. Your black eyes will always give you away.' To

*this day I have never wanted anything that belonged to some-
one else."*

(My great-grandmother was talking about the color of my
grandmother's eyes. My mother inherited the same color eyes,
and I did as well, though I always called mine "chocolate." It
seemed less intense.)

I've always been in awe of the way my parents were able
to teach us lessons individually, depending on what level of
understanding we were at. Every one of my brothers has a
personal story of how Mother was able to give them a good
moral education, with some type of parable or metaphor, without ever being patronizing or humiliating. My mother's favorite animal character was always an owl. She used it as the
logo on the stationery for her business, a small publishing company called Knowledge Unlimited, with the scriptural ref-
erence of "Oh, Be Wise." One of the owl's greatest attributes
is that it can see small things happening, even in the dark of
night.

The same was true of my mother. She could recognize any
emotional storm that was clouding our perspectives because of
unwise choices we had made, even the smallest indiscretion.
Mothers all have some level of intuition, but the wisdom of my
mother was that she refined hers. She worked her intuition
like a muscle, never dismissing its importance in being a good
parent.

I, on the other hand, have had to learn to develop my intuition by giving myself space and time to listen to it. I have had
a hard time in the past balancing the ability to constantly pay

attention with being able to have fun with my kids. About twelve years ago, we were in Orlando for the Children's Miracle Network Celebration. After we wrapped up the event, I decided to take the kids to Disney World for the day before we flew back to Utah.

Brandon and Brianna were still toddlers, so I pushed along a double stroller and stood by as the older kids all rode the rides together. Late in the afternoon, I told each of the kids that they could pick out one souvenir from a gift store before we left for the hotel. As Jessica, Rachael, and Mike were all showing me different styles of hats, watches, T-shirts, and fun pajamas, little did I know that the two babies were filling the basket underneath their stroller with anything that caught their eye at my knee level. Before we checked out, I pushed the stroller to the stuffed-toy section and let them each pick out one toy. Imagine my surprise when the security guard stopped me at the door and said, "Ms. Osmond, you'll also have to pay for all the product in the stroller." I bent down to look under the stroller at a basket almost full of key chains, bracelets, pens, luggage tags and small toys. A small crowd started to gather as they realized who it was the guard had stopped at the door. Some people started to shake their heads. I couldn't believe it.

It sounds unconvincing that I hadn't noticed my toddlers putting about twenty-five items in the stroller, but that's exactly what happened. Of course, I replaced all the items on their hooks, all the while feeling somewhat embarrassed and, I have to admit, somewhat amused. Sure, I thought, I take one tiny elephant in my foray into criminal activity, but not my kids. They wipe out the inventory! Good thing Twitter and Facebook weren't invented yet! I always teach my kids to think big if they're going to pursue something. I guess they took it seriously.

I could see the press release in my head: "Marie Osmond, cofounder of the largest children's charity, raises $3 billion for Children's Miracle Network and then pilfers $150 worth of Disney trinkets from the gift store."

When we got back to the hotel, I decided to tell Brandon and Brianna the story of Vera's dime, but soon remembered that neither one of them was old enough to know what a dime was. However, I realized that day that even toddlers, besides being able to recognize hundreds of corporate logos, are able to differentiate right from wrong. Why else would they have put the items in the basket under the stroller where I wouldn't see them? Somewhere in their consciences, they knew that they were doing something they shouldn't have been doing. I have the strong feeling that we truly are born with an internal moral compass. It's the desires and dictates of a confusing world that redirect the needle in that compass.

My mother also taught each of us accountability when it came to taking care of our own possessions. But being the headstrong child that I was, I had to learn that one the hard way, too. When I was about seven years old, my mother bought me a pair of sparkly patent leather shoes with imitation jewels all over them. I thought they were spectacularly gorgeous, as only a little girl who loved ultrafeminine attire would, and I couldn't wait to wear them. She advised me to save them to wear for special occasions and to church on Sundays, but I thought she was being overly cautious. At first, I just wore them around the house, my eyes glued to my amazing feet everywhere I walked.

Then the great outdoors beckoned. My brothers were taking turns riding the little tractor in the field and I wanted to join them. The combination of a freshly plowed field that had been rained on the night before and gem-covered shoes is not a good one. The field will always dominate.

When it was time to come back in the house for dinner, I couldn't even wear my prized shoes inside anymore. The patent leather had been scratched deeply by rocks, the soles were soaked with mud, and dirt had clogged every empty space between the gems. They were a mess. And I had only owned them for two days! When my mother finally saw them left on the step by the back door, I thought I would be in trouble. She just shook her head and shrugged. "That's too bad," she told me. "Now you'll have to wear your old shoes to church and to anything special." Again, in my headstrong determination, I thought I could correct the situation and prove my mother wrong. I found a scrub brush and tried to clean them up, but the brush only scratched the patent leather more and the dirt was ground more deeply into the gemstones and some even popped out of their settings. It was hopeless.

My mother stood by her word (even though I'm sure it was just as hard for her to take her only girl to church in old, well-worn shoes); there would be no new shoes for what seemed like a long, long time. It was probably just a couple of months, but it was enough time for the lesson to stick firmly in my head. Maybe this is why I love great shoes to this day!

When one of my younger sons was in sixth grade, he and a schoolmate had a science project and for the presentation decided to wear a costume that demonstrated their theory. This costume involved gold-colored shoes. His buddy found an old pair of sneakers that he no longer wore and spray-painted them gold.

My son forgot to look for something he could use and at the last minute ended up spray-painting his brand-new tennis shoes with the gold paint. After the presentation, my son came home from school and made his case that I should take him out right away to get replacement shoes, since the sneakers had been ruined for a school project.

He was surprised when I said, "Oh, no. I'm not going to spend another eighty-five dollars on new shoes. I just bought you that pair last week."

He protested in full that it was unfair and he didn't have a choice.

I explained as logically as I could, seeing the rising panic on his face. "My son, you knew for a whole week that you were going to need gold shoes for this project. You didn't have to ruin your brand-new shoes. You made that choice, so now you have to live with the consequences of your decision."

And he did. I must admit I felt a bit bad for him as he went out the door to school every day looking like the FTD floral delivery guy. Lucky for him, he had a major growth spurt within a couple months and needed new shoes.

One of my most difficult mothering moments happened when my oldest daughter, Jessica, was eighteen years old. She had finished high school and was trying to figure out what to do next in life. In the meantime, she had met a new group of friends who had been raised in a radically different environment from the one Jessica had been raised in. They were allowed to "party" at home and didn't seem to have restrictions on any activities they chose to participate in.

Whatever the appeal was to Jessica, she decided that she wanted to find a job in southern California where this group of friends lived. I was hoping for a different choice, but since she was eighteen years old, I had to let her go. Even Jessica's closest siblings, when they met this group of friends, tried to warn her that they could tell these friends felt no loyalty.

I helped Jessica buy a used car, and we shopped for items for her apartment there, which she was sharing with a couple of the other girls. I flew down to see her place and to take her out to dinner, spending the night on the couch in her room. Jessica found a job, but it all went downhill quickly. As it turned out, she was spending any money she made on entertaining these friends, as well as on buying food and clothing.

She brought a couple of these friends to my home for a visit, and I discovered later that one girl had stolen one of my designer purses from my closet as well as a gift card I had been given. They also brought alcohol into my home while I was gone on a two-day business trip, which is absolutely forbidden. When I asked Jessica about it over the phone, she denied that any of it could be possible and was angry with me for accusing her good friends of stealing.

I had to tell her that her friends would no longer be allowed in the house. Jessica was not happy about it, but she was still not ready to admit that these kids were using her purposely. I missed my daughter, but I knew that it would only end in resentment if I tried to convince her to leave this group behind and come back home. A couple of times she called me to say she didn't have enough money to buy food or put gas in her car. I would send her a check, but I was never convinced that she used it for herself. Mostly, she was trying to stay in the group by having something to offer. If I dared to express my concerns about her friends, she would defend them and then shut me out. About three months later, when Jessica had been laid off from her job and had no expendable income, her friends decided that they no longer wanted to share an apartment with her. They staged some type of complaint against her and then Jessica found herself out of a living situation; she had nothing but her boxes of belongings in her car. I was driving to work when I got a phone call from my daughter. She told me she didn't have any place to live, or a job, or even enough money to buy gas to get home.

I listened and then knew that I had to make a decision and that it was going to be painful.

If I enabled her by sending her money, she would probably go back to her group of friends with the money as a peace offering. I could tell she wasn't thinking clearly because she still didn't perceive how much her tender heart was being manipulated by this group. I chose to be there for her as a listener, but to remain silent in offering a solution. Finally she said, "What am I supposed to do, sell my computer and iPod for gas money?"

My heart ached knowing how I had to answer. I said, "I guess so. You made the choice to be there and to spend your money on them. I've given you money and had my purse and gift card stolen from me. I don't want to enable your friends anymore." Jessica fell silent. After a couple minutes more, she said she was going to have to go figure out where she could sell her belongings. I let her hang up the phone, feeling terrible for her. Those of you who have gone through it know that the tough-love approach is much tougher on the mother.

A few minutes later, I called a girlfriend who knows all of my kids to talk to her about my decision. She was sympathetic to my pain, but she also thought I had made the right choice. "The law of nature in the animal kingdom is for the young to become independent of the mother, so they need survival skills," she gently pointed out. "Even so, very few young animals learn to fend for themselves willingly. For two years bear cubs will stay with their mother and let her do all the hard work for them. The mother bear has to become ferocious and run them up a tree. When the cubs have the courage to come down, she is long gone and they have to make do on their own." The approach is tough and most likely a bit heartbreaking for the mama bear, but necessary to the survival of her offspring. My own mother certainly ran me up a tree a few times. And now I can honestly say that I've always been able to take care of myself.

I was still worried to the core about what Jes would do next. I knew that she didn't have a place to go and that she would probably have to spend the night in her car or find another friend who would let her sleep on her couch. I knew she was really mad at me for not helping her out in her desperation. But I also knew that this would be a deciding factor in my child's life. Would she wake up to her self-worth, or would she allow herself to be directed by the whims of those who would lead her down a dead-end street?

That night, I didn't sleep at all. I kept checking my phone to see if she had called again.

She hadn't.

Early the next morning, I called my friend Patty, who lives in LA. She was about a forty-five-minute drive from where Jessica had been staying. I told her what was going on, and she offered to call Jessica. I knew Jessica would take Patty's phone call. It was such a relief to me when Patty said she had talked to her and would be seeing her that day.

A while later, a very humble young woman called me to apologize and on her next visit arrived carrying in her hand my missing designer bag. After we had hung up the phone that night, she had found a place to sell her iPod and gotten enough money to put gas in her car. She had gone back to her friend's place that night and searched out my stolen purse, confronting the girl for the truth. She managed to leave with it and also regain a bit of self-esteem. She drove back to Utah, straight through, and stayed temporarily at the house we have there until she could find a job and get her own place again.

There are bumps in the road for all of us as we grow up and

struggle to find our identity, but that phone call was truly a turning point for us both. I respected her for having the courage to recover my stolen property, even when her heart was so bruised by this group of friends, and she respected that I had drawn a boundary about helping her continue on a life path that held no promise.

In the years since then, my daughter has been a good teacher for her four youngest siblings. She can tell them of experiences that they think are way out of my realm.

And that's okay with me, as long as they get the message that keeps them from making bad choices.

In the same way that my parents held us accountable for our gifts, our possessions, and our actions, even more so they held us accountable for our words. If we said we would do something, we had to follow through. Our handshake was our contract. My mom even held us accountable for the words we said about ourselves. She believed that words have a powerful energy. Whenever I had a low-self-esteem day and said something negative about my looks, my body, or my intellectual ability, she would stop me in my tracks; she wouldn't let me proceed until I said three things that I liked about myself. It embarrassed me, and it would take me a while to come up with three things. That was the point she was trying to make. It's too easy to talk badly about yourself and can be hard to stop once you start. So don't even start.

Mostly, my mother was always making sure we didn't spread harmful lies or gossip about others.

I always wondered why my mother almost always wore a

wig anytime she had to be in public. She wore them shopping and every day when we were out on tour. She wore them to church and when she went to business meetings. I used to joke that being on a tour bus with eight boys and all the male band members, who would kick off their shoes to relax, my mother had to stick her head out of the window for fresh air; then when the bus stopped, she didn't have to worry about her hair, which had been blown about for hours, as long as she had a wig she could plop on.

When I asked her about it later in her life, I heard the real story. She told me that she used to go to the beauty parlor once a week to have her hair done, but she always felt bad when she left because the women in the salon always gossiped about other women and spoke so badly about their husbands or in-laws or neighbors; it was like a dark cloud would descend on her usually happy spirit. She couldn't understand how women could betray one another and also their spouses in such a harsh way, saying things that, if repeated, could have destroyed families. She didn't want to hear it anymore, so she stopped going to a salon.

One windy summer day when I was a young girl, my mother was changing out our old bedding for new pillows and sheets. She decided to demonstrate for us the importance of the ninth commandment, which is "Thou shalt not bear false witness against thy neighbor." She got the idea from a folktale that had been around since the nineteenth century. The story has been retold with different characters in various cultures, but the message is always the same.

My mother cut open an old feather pillow and let us each have a go at shaking the feathers out into the wind. We loved it. Then she told us: "Think of those feathers as your words. Each one is something you say to someone or about them, both good and bad. Now, go and pick up all the feathers that are loose."

We looked at my mother like she was crazy. The feathers had blown far and wide, across the yard and the road and into the surrounding fields.

"You would never be able to get them all back. Right?"

I was glad that she seemed to be coming to her senses. Of course, it was an impossible task.

She smiled at us and said, "Those feathers scattered everywhere are what it's like when you gossip or speak badly about another person. Once it leaves your mouth, you can never get it back, no matter how hard you may try or how much you regret saying it. Whoever heard it may repeat it to another, who tells another, and on and on. So guard your words well, because they can either hurt others greatly or be kind and gentle and uplifting."

As I was writing this, I thought it would be a great lesson to carry forward with my younger kids now. We could drive to the top of one of the foothills surrounding Las Vegas and tear open a pillow. The only issue is, I'll have to go find an old feather pillow somewhere other than my house. My kids are so attached to their individual feather pillows, it would be like sacrificing a favorite pair of jeans. The message would definitely be lost.

One of the last entries in my mother's journals was about

accountability. I didn't read this until after she had passed away: "*For the virtue of accountability to return, parents must teach by example, showing their children the importance of this powerful virtue. . . . If not, it will continue to lead to destroyed lives. All truths, self and otherwise, will be abandoned by the next generation, a phenomenon we have observed throughout history, leading to nothing but sorrow. I fear for this outcome, and it breaks my heart.*"

We are raising our children in verbally harsh times. The political commercials in which professional adults call one another liars and cheats must be confusing to children who hear them. We seem to live in a culture that celebrates "getting away with something" or twisting the truth to fit our needs, rationalizing our wasting of time, resources, and talents instead of holding ourselves to a higher moral standard. Just look at how we've declined as a society. It seems that people only feel bad about a misdeed if they get caught at it.

Like my mother, I "fear for this outcome," too. I want my children to be able to live in a world where your word counts for something and where they understand and appreciate that the gifts they've been given are to be shared and that people always come before possessions. But I also know that, like my mother before me, my husband and I need to be a living example of accountability to our children. It isn't always easy. Sometimes I just want to say to my kids, "Because I said so" or "Do what I say, not what I do." However, I doubt any child in history has ever thought that was a truthful or convincing reason to live with integrity.

Above the desk where I'm writing hangs a mother's quilt I made with my daughter and some close girlfriends after my mother passed away. I wanted to have a way to display the things that meant the most to my mother. One square is a family tree because she loved genealogy; another is a baby dress that her only daughter had worn. There is a square containing the last cross-stitch she was working on, still in the hoop with the needle in the same place she left it. Another section has a black-and-white photo of my parents on their wedding day. Underneath the photo is the treasured string of pearls she wore with her wedding dress, the ones that her own mother had given to her and that she had passed along to me. One of my girlfriends suggested that we embroider one of the sayings that my mother loved and quoted often. I didn't have to think for very long about which one it would be. She always had this taped up somewhere in the house: "Character is doing what's right even when no one is watching."

My own children love to look at the quilt and hear stories about her. She taught by example and lived her own teachings. She was always accountable for her actions and her words. She raised eight boys who are good and loving men, devoted to their families. And she raised me. I know I've made far more mistakes than my mother did, but I can only hope that one day my own children will tell their babies and grandbabies a good story about accountability that they learned from me.

I also wonder, looking up at the quilt, if my mother ever spit on that string of pearls.

She owned them, so I think I know the answer.

Accountability

The willingness to take full responsibility for our choices.

$\mathscr{L}$ISTEN

KIM GOODWIN

*I love my family ferociously. At my son's wedding, 2011: (from left)
Brandon, Matthew, Rachael, Steve, Claire, Stephen, me, Abigail,
Brianna, and Jessica.*

"We thought she was long gone," a southern California cattle rancher said about one of his all-time favorite cows. For over twenty years, he owned a ranch with almost four thousand acres, near the San Bernardino Mountains. He had bought the cow, he told my mother, right after she gave birth to her first calf, and since then, she had given birth to fourteen more, about one calf every year. Her offspring were always born healthy and sturdy, which made her a cow of great value. Then one day she didn't return from the pasture to the barn with the others. The rancher's farmhands drove across most of the property in a Jeep to see if she had strayed or was injured, but returned without a single clue as to what happened to this cow.

The rancher said, "I was sad about it. She was getting older, so I thought some kind of wildlife had caught up to her, but we didn't find remains. It was kind of a mystery."

A couple of months later, the rancher and some helpers went out on their twice-a-year trek on horseback to make sure all of the fences on the property were still standing and in good condition. In one remote section was a steep rocky incline that the rancher usually just rode past on his way to the far corner fence. One of the farmhands pointed out a tree that seemed to be growing at the top of it, which was unusual. Out of curiosity, the rancher coaxed his horse up the tricky slope to see about the tree and how it could possibly grow up there on the solid rock. At the top, where no one had ventured before, the rancher found to his surprise a plateau about the size of a large yard. It had become layered with enough dirt to grow grass. A deep hollowed-out place in the rock had filled with rainwater, which had become a nature-made pond. And growing next to it was one tree. What made the scene even more surreal was that standing under that tree was the missing cow. The rancher said that his jaw dropped down to his horse's saddle at the sight of the cow he thought he'd never see again. He couldn't imagine how the cow had found her way there, especially since his horse had had trouble getting up the rocky incline.

"She wasn't all that happy to see me," the rancher recalled. "When I walked toward her, she hustled herself away to the farthest grassy edge. She turned to look at me like I had discovered her secret hideaway."

"What did you do?" my mother had asked him. "How did you get her down from there?"

The rancher laughed and shook his head.

"I didn't," he said. "Cows don't talk, but she was sending me a message loud and clear. I had to listen. She wanted time to herself. There was plenty of grass and water for one cow to live on, and she had the tree for shade. I had to hand it to her:

She had found the perfect getaway. I figured she had already given me the best fifteen years of her life. I couldn't ask her to leave the patch of private paradise she had found on her own. Who was I to interfere?"

I love this real-life story. When I pass it along to other women, especially mothers, they love it, too. I think it's because we can all relate to the need for a private space. It's not that we want to retire and live a solitary life away from our families and children. It's more that we want time to refill the well so that we have more to give to others. Most women I know have to work really hard, navigating a slippery slope of schedule, expectations, and obligations, to find one little plot of space where they can have time that is all their own. Like the runaway cow, the women I know don't need a luxurious space, just a quiet one with guilt-free time to replenish our spirits. It could be a sewing room, the gym, or even sitting on a blanket under a tree with a good book.

When I was growing up, there were a couple of weekends when my brothers and my father went off on a business or fishing trip and my mother and I would have the house to ourselves for two peaceful days. It hardly ever happened, so when it did, we would both take full advantage of the quiet. We would even give each other plenty of space, going to opposite ends of the house and only meeting up for meals. I thought an uninterrupted nap was the greatest gift I could give to my mother. I know for sure now that I was right, because it's about the greatest gift I can receive at this point in my life, too!

When your kids are young, it's rare to have five minutes to

yourself, even in the bathtub, without a knock on the door. When they are a bit older, their activities can fill every spare hour of the week, which doesn't include making sure the basic necessities are taken care of: healthy meals, clean clothes, medical and dental needs, and the list goes on. Most mothers I know can feel like they are so busy "doing" life that they are no longer "living" life. Life can go by faster and faster, but be less and less fulfilling.

You've probably seen the ongoing parenting discussion on the Internet, at church, at school, and in various groups on the subject of quality time versus quantity time with kids. What I've learned raising my own eight children is that they don't want quantity or quality time as any adult might define it. Children want ALL of your time. And by "time" I mean your undivided, uninterrupted attention. They really aren't counting the minutes that you spend with them in comparison to others. What they are measuring is how much they feel listened to and acknowledged. All of my memories from my childhood have to do with a feeling or an emotion, not with the hour on the clock or the day of the week. If you think about it, you may find that it's true for you, as well.

As an adult, I realized that my respect for my mother was deeply rooted at a young age because of the way she gave each of us her undivided attention when we needed her the most. With nine children, it was impossible to give us equal amounts of time, but she somehow managed to make each of us feel understood, cared about, and even uniquely special. Those qualities transcended the amount of time on the clock. If you had my mother's attention, you had it fully. She could accomplish in five minutes, through the act of attentive listening, what we contemporary mothers constantly struggle to do; we feel we are basically robbing our children of our undivided attention. My mother was able to make us feel remarkably safe and whole again just through the act of simple listening and caring, even when we became adults. In my mother's journals from 1992, she wrote about one of my brothers coming over, upset about an argument with his wife: *"I didn't say much at all. He only seemed to want my undivided attention. That's what I gave him. I listened to everything he wanted to tell me. Afterwards [he] took a nap. He seemed to feel better when he left. Bless his heart."*

On the "Mother's quilt" I made to commemorate her life, which hangs in my house, I embroidered the aphorism that my mom used as a template to raise each one of us. She had also written it into her journal in the 1960s and sent it out to readers of her Mother Osmond newsletters in the 1980s to all of our fans. This is it:

Mother's Recipe for a Happy Child

> *A pinch of humor*
> *A dash of patience*
> *A hint of friendship*
> *A sprinkle of listening*
> *A slice of kindness*
> *Mix in love and bake with example*

Notice the quantities prescribed to help your child be happy: a pinch, a dash, and a sprinkle. Not a gallon of guilt for their normal childhood growing pains, or a bushel of bargaining for your child's affection because you need her to be your friend, or a pound of self-punishment for comparing yourself to other mothers and feeling like you can't compete.

Because my mother knew that she couldn't be there 24-7 for each of her children, she instilled in us the self-worth to believe we could make good decisions and wise choices on our own. That was a key gift she gave to each of us with love. And she and my father stood at the periphery of our lives to lend support when we might need it. He was another constant and steady presence for all of us, his children.

One afternoon when my two oldest children were little and my mother was visiting, we watched as Stephen played LEGOs on the floor with Jessica. Holding baby Rachael on her lap, my mother said to me: "I remember doing this when I was your age. I was sitting in the living room watching Alan, Wayne, and Merrill play with Lincoln Logs on the carpet, holding baby Jay in my arms. I thought this is how God must view all of us: as little children, working to design and build up our lives, trying to make something for ourselves out of all of the toy pieces. And He is watching over us with love, helping us to grow, but not interfering with our free will unless we ask."

My mother lived the example of what it meant to respect another by listening with an open heart and without judgment. From the time we could first understand, she explained about free will and agency. She said that we would each have many opportunities to make millions of choices. But we would also have to live with the consequences of those choices, so she hoped we would make wise choices and use discernment.

She would tell us that choosing is what separates us from every other living thing. You can choose how you're going to let something affect your life, for both good and bad. You may not be able to change your life overnight, but you can choose to take a small step today and then take another tomorrow.

She would rarely say: "I'm so proud of you." Instead she would say: "Aren't you proud of yourself? Don't you feel good about your accomplishment?" She validated our feelings, our opinions, and our perspectives, and, in the bigger picture, our individual spirits.

As much as my mother loved technology and the fast-forward advances in communicating electronically (she was one of the first people I knew who owned a personal computer in the early 1980s, long before it was common), I think she would have felt sadness for this generation of children because of our current reliance on technology. Many of us seem to depend on staying in touch with the world by always having a cell phone in our hand or nearby. My mother would often say, "You have so much stress with everything that you have to keep up with now: your businesses, your touring and speaking schedules, trying to oversee Children's Miracle Network, and everyone expecting an instant answer to every question by e-mail. On top of that, being a mother. I can't imagine how you do it all."

I don't think we can "do it all" well. We may be staying in touch with the world, but are we losing touch in our homes?

My cell phone is many things to me. It's my movable office, my link to any news I might need, my GPS in the car, my way to listen to recordings I'm working on, and mostly my connection to my older kids and friends. So I admit that I feel uncomfortable without it nearby. Between texting, updating social media, checking in on the hundreds of e-mails I get every day, calendar notifications, and reminders, it seems like I'm always looking down at the phone in my hand. I know I'm not alone in this because almost all of the women around me are doing the same thing, even if they are using an app to keep track of what they need at the store. As much as the technology has simplified our adult lives, I believe it has started to complicate and even damage our relationships with our children.

I'm a woman who is a mega-multitasker, because I have to be one. The "to-do" list of my life every day is longer than what could possibly get done in the hours of that day. Like many other women I know, I've evolved to the point where I can combine tasks and still keep track of it all. I really am capable of hearing what my child is saying to me even while I'm answering a text from a producer and packing for a concert tour or press trip. I can almost always repeat back to my child what he or she has been telling me. However, just because I can doesn't mean that it's the right thing to do. I know that multitasking is not how my children feel my love for them. I've come to realize that children need eye-to-eye contact with their parents, just like we do as adults with one another. Think about it: We don't go see movies about people staring down at a text message or gazing for two hours at a computer screen. We want to watch their eye contact and dialogue, the emotion of human interaction. It's true with children, too.

A business associate told me about a day she was doing some online banking on her smartphone while her preschool-age son was playing a game on the floor nearby. It was her only time to catch up on household matters, and she felt under constant pressure to keep current with everything. When her little son said, "Watch this, Mommy," she would glance over at him and smile and then try to finish her banking transaction. She said she didn't even realize that her child was frustrated until he appeared at her elbow and took her face in his small hands and pleaded, "Play with me with your eyes, Mommy."

It broke her heart. From then on, after she left work for the day, she put the phone away until after she had tucked her son into bed for the night. His happiness and calmness increased by leaps and bounds. She told me that her own sense of well-being and self-worth as a mother increased, as well.

When my daughter Brianna was two years old, I was driving to the TV studio to work and multitasking by returning phone calls as the car sat in traffic on the 101 freeway in Los Angeles. This was before it became illegal to drive and talk on a handheld cell phone.

Brianna kept reaching from her car seat in the back and whimpering for me to give her the phone as I inched along, bumper to bumper. Finally, the traffic started to move and pick up speed, so I finished my last call and I reached back to hand

Brianna the phone to let her pretend to talk on it. But she didn't want to play with the phone; she wanted to get rid of it. In the rearview mirror, I caught my daughter's one swift move as she launched the phone out the open window. It crashed to the asphalt in the next lane to be immediately run over by an approaching car.

I couldn't believe it! (And this was 1999, when a cell phone was still around six hundred dollars!) But it opened my eyes that day. And my ears. Now when the kids are in the car with me, I try to put the phone down and use the time to talk with them. It's a great way to have personal time with each child, and being in a car together provides a good atmosphere for listening. It's not always easy, because—let's be real—hearing the play-by-play of what happened during volleyball in gym class, or a detailed description of the progression and number of times Justin Bieber has changed his hairstyle in the last six months, can be enough to make my eyes glaze over (I feel for the mothers in the past who had to hear about Donny nonstop), but the contentment on my kids' faces makes it worthwhile. Usually after the events of the day are discussed, the topic will turn to something of more substance. If I am quiet and listen, they will eventually come around to talking about the concerns that are making them worry or the hopes of their hearts.

My mom and I had some of our most profound mother-daughter talks when we were riding in tour buses from show to show. I would tell her everything that was going on for me; she would comfort my insecurities and encourage my dreams.

I'm sure she would have appreciated having that time to put her head back and rest for a while, but that rarely happened. She was always checking in with one of her children.

I often think of how many other demands there were on my mother's time.

It must have been challenging for her to have to be our teacher, not only of values and life skills, but also our correspondence lessons. She had to figure out ways to teach us on tour buses, airplanes, vans, and hotel rooms or in cramped quarters backstage and even make it fun to learn. For example, she wrote in a journal from 1975: *"Jimmy and I sat together on the bus going back to Brussels and worked on memorizing a few more of the states by association. 'Calls a fawn into the ark . . . California. Calls a rat a doe . . . Colorado. The doe cut his toe and had to connect it . . . Connecticut.'"*

After an exhausting day of doing two shows, pressing and repairing costumes, packing bags, and figuring out how to keep us all healthy on the road, I'm sure making up a game for a nine-year-old to learn the states wasn't something she felt like doing. But she did it. And I'm betting that my brother Jimmy can still recite all of the associations she created to remember each state, because my mother made it feel like special time.

We were often in situations like press events, TV show tapings, or backstage where we weren't supposed to talk or make noise. From the time we were very young, my mother started a secret code with us. She would squeeze our hands or our arms three times to represent the words "I love you." It was a physical reminder of her constant presence and affection for each of us. Until two days before she passed away, she was still able to move her hand enough to squeeze mine three times. Words were not necessary. The message was there, as it always had been. I've passed this code along to my children, who now squeeze my hand three times.

My mother was the person everyone could count on to listen. It wasn't only her own children who would tell her their joys and concerns; she received letters from sad and confused teenagers from around the world who would refer to her as "Mother Osmond." She would write back to them about everything from a simple suggestion of how to act on a first date to the most complicated of emotional situations, like living with a neglectful or alcoholic parent. Over the course of my life, especially the past ten years, I've had countless numbers of women and men come up to me to say that having "Mother Osmond" in their lives was what got them through their adolescence. Many of them kept a correspondence going with my mother until she passed away. She would keep files of their letters and always loved to get photos in the mail of their graduations, marriages, babies, and lives. She called them all her "other" children, and they were the reason she started her M.O.M. (Mother Osmond's Memo), the newsletter she mailed around the world to hundreds of fans. When the Internet came along, she was ecstatic that she could e-mail her letters to so many more; her subscriber base grew into the thousands. Even then, she always wrote the newsletters in the same style, as if she were talking to a loved one, updating people on marriages and births in the Osmond family, sharing great ideas, inspirational stories, and insights she wanted to pass along. She had a lifelong interest in any ideas that would give people more happiness, hope, and peace of mind. She was a New Age thinker long before the term even became popular. She had a natural understanding of what is now known as the power of quantum physics: that even the smallest thought or action creates a momentum of energy. It supported her steadfast quest to teach us to always apply positive thinking to every situation. She was only interested in thoughts to move us forward.

When I was doing the *Donny & Marie* television show as a young teenager, my mother gave me the idea to write a book for girls called *Marie Osmond's Guide to Beauty, Health, and Style*. As my mother explained it to me, she was getting hundreds of letters from girls from broken homes where the mother had to work full-time. The girls had so little time with their own mothers, they needed direction on even the basic matters that they should have been learning at home, like how to keep their clothing in order or even how to shave their legs. My mother's tender heart ached for these girls, who seemed to have no one to guide them.

As I mention in my 2009 book, *Might As Well Laugh About It Now*, even Elvis Presley would call and talk for hours to my mother on the phone. He had lost his own mother a few years earlier, and when he met my mother backstage at a Las Vegas show, he asked if he could call her. The calls would last for over an hour, with my mother pulling the phone into another room for privacy. As a little girl, I would often try to sit next to the door, or casually walk through the room, to see if

I could overhear what my mother was saying to Elvis Presley. As soon as she figured out I was there, she would shoo me away. A few years later, my mother grieved the day she heard of his death, heartbroken that such a tenderhearted man and huge talent had passed away so young. I asked my mother what Elvis would say to her when they talked. She told me that he would ask her for advice, talk to her about God's wisdom in the Scriptures, and tell her his deepest concerns.

Of course, no one in our family got to hear even one detail about Elvis's questions or concerns, because my mother never shared any of his private information. His trust in my mother was immense, but his intuition was on target. He knew he was putting his trust in the right person. Always, following one of their lengthy phone calls, a huge bouquet of roses would arrive for my mother. She was happy to be there for him, but it wasn't because he was Elvis Presley. She would have done the same thing if one of the stagehands in Vegas had asked if she would listen to him.

My mother was a good listener, which made her a great healer.

No matter where my mother lived, she tried to be socially connected to her community. She would chat over a backyard fence with the neighbor, in the hallways of the church, or in the aisle at the market.

She knew who was going through a hard time, because she asked her neighbors how they were doing whenever she saw them. If she knew they were having a tough day, she would do little things to bring them comfort, like put a basket of homemade bread or muffins on their porch or fresh cut flowers or berries from her garden. She was always aware but would never interfere. She seemed to intuitively know what to do.

My mother would often say to us as children, "Never allow the spirit of contention to enter your thoughts. If you can't say something nice, don't say anything at all." I've shortened that for my own children. I just say, "Zip it." Times have changed!

She once told me, when I asked her why she would never talk about anyone in a negative way, ever: "I could have destroyed families with the things that people would tell me privately. Why would I ever do that? They trusted me."

Even though I spent much of my childhood thinking that my mother was perfect, I know she wasn't. None of us is. If she acted in a way that seemed perfect, it was because she used wisdom through her constant search for a better understanding of everything from horticulture to teaching the hearing impaired, from genealogy to child psychology, and applied what she had learned.

One of the quotes she would pin up on the wall is attributed to a famous British preacher from the mid-1800s, Charles Spurgeon: "Wisdom is the proper application of knowledge." Today, there is an abundance of knowledge available, but the question is: Are we learning the wisdom necessary to apply it correctly?

My mother was passionate about one thing that, due to the circumstances of our "on-the-go" lives, she could rarely achieve: organization, or as her own mother would call it "everything in apple pie order." She was always happiest when she could set up new files or ways to store information, recipes, and ideas. In the 1970s, she wrote a book called *Let's Get Organized*, which thousands of fans purchased.

She liked the idea of always knowing where everything was, but that became impossible with our touring and moving numerous times over the years.

One thing that she would consistently do, no matter where we traveled, toured, visited, or lived, was to write out a list of what she wanted to do that day. At the top of that list, without fail, was one word: "Prayer." Before anyone else got up in the morning, she would sit at a table in the quiet for about thirty minutes and read her Scriptures; she would pray for direction to any problems and give thanks for her blessings. That usually meant that she slept only three or four hours every night, rarely getting to catch an extra few winks to make it through her long days. She always felt like prayer would sustain her far more than the sleep she lost.

I know that prayer, meditation, and study were how my mother "refilled the well." It set the tone for her day and reminded her that she didn't have to struggle alone, that she could trust in guidance from God, if she would take the time each day to listen to His direction.

When I was about nine years old, I asked my mother why she believed in God. Without hesitation, she told me, "Because He answers my prayers."

Then she told me a story of how, very early in her life, she had had an experience of what it meant to listen and pay attention to the messages God sends.

As a little girl, she lived with her parents in a tiny home near a canal in Idaho. After a huge snowfall, my mother took her sled outside and climbed a hill behind their house. The snow seemed to pile high on the edge of the hill, so my mother eagerly moved to the very top to get the most mileage on the slide down. As she got near, she heard a voice say, "Go back, Olive! Turn around and walk back down the hill!" My mother said she looked around, startled, because she knew no one else could have been up there with her and she had never heard a voice like that. She decided to listen to the advice and walked down the side of the hill instead of using her sled. Out of curiosity, once she was safely down, she looked back up to what she thought was the slope of the hill. It was only a false snow ledge, about a foot thick, that had been created by the blowing winds. It hung out over a big hollowed-out space above a twelve-foot drop to the snow-covered ground below. She knew then that if she had walked to the edge with her sled, she would have fallen through and been injured or buried alive until spring. She felt that she had been guarded by angels and was grateful she had listened.

From that time on, the verse from Psalms "Be still and know that I am God" had more meaning to my mother. It was one of the first Scripture verses she taught my brothers and me.

I had a number of incidents in my own life when, by following my mother's advice about "listening" to my own intuition, I was able to get instructions that saved me from danger.

When Stephen was a baby, we were staying in a condo in Los Angeles. My husband, Steve, was working, so my girlfriend

Tina was with me to help care for our son while I was dealing with a long day of various TV and press appearances I had to do for work. We returned to the condo after dark that evening, tired and hungry.

Starting as a child, I had developed a couple of customary habits from living in so many different places and staying in hundreds of different hotel rooms my entire life. One habit is I always open every closet door in every room and leave them open. The other is: Before I enter any place I'm staying that night, I have an automatic internal dialogue with God, asking that all will be safe and secure. Returning to the LA condo that evening, Tina helped me bring in a couple bags of groceries, while I carried Stephen in his car seat into the house. Usually, the first thing I would do after getting home is take the baby from his car seat and carry him upstairs with me to get him changed and into pajamas. For some reason, I left him in his car seat and asked Tina if she would warm his bottle up while I went upstairs for his pajamas. As I walked up the stairs, I had a strong feeling of alarm come over me. I didn't know why at first, until I turned the corner to go into the bedroom and noticed the closet doors; they were both closed. I knew there wasn't a chance that Steve had been back home. I felt a cold apprehension, and my heart started to race. It was obvious to me that I needed to get out quick, but I also sensed a prompting by the spirit that it would be very dangerous to let the intruder know that I was aware of his presence. Doing the best I could to keep my voice sounding casual, I said out loud, as if talking to myself, "Oh, I forgot my purse."

I spun around and headed back down the stairs. I signaled to Tina in the kitchen not to say anything, to turn off the stove and follow me. I lifted the baby's car seat from off the floor, and we stepped as quietly as possible back out the front door. Once outside on the porch, I put in the house key and locked the door behind me. I remember thinking how unusual it was for me to feel prompted to lock the apartment since all I wanted to do was get away quickly. Tina, even though she had no idea what I was doing, could see the urgency in my face and had started to buckle Stephen's car seat back into the car. We jumped into the car and locked the doors, and I drove away from the house as fast as I safely could. Not knowing what to do, I stopped at a public phone where I called my in-laws, who lived about fifteen minutes away. They called the police, who said they would go to the condo to check out the situation. My in-laws told me they'd be there as soon as possible and to meet them back at my condo but not until after the police had been there first.

The police said when they arrived they found the front door ajar, but no one was inside and nothing seemed to be disturbed. When I asked them if the closet doors were open or closed upstairs, they said open. I told them the doors were closed when I was in the apartment. The police concluded that this intruder was hiding in the closet and obviously meant to do me physical harm. As frightening as the idea was, I also felt gratitude that I had listened to my intuition and paid attention.

The experiences that have caused me the most concern or heartache as a mother have always occurred when I ignored

the voice of my intuition. In May 2008, I was touring internationally with my brothers for their fiftieth-anniversary tour. I
was a single mother at that time, so I had my four younger
children, then ages five to eleven, with me. Jimmy and his wife
also had their four children with them, and Donny's wife, Debbie, and their two younger sons were also along. During the
day, we would often take all of the kids sightseeing because it
was a great educational opportunity.

Traveling with our family was a longtime friend and personal assistant who still works with me and is an incredible
help on many levels. She's a trusted friend who keeps us all
organized and running efficiently. She knew my mother well
for about twenty years, and the two of them were like organi-
zational clones!

Near the end of our tour, we had a scheduled show at the
famous Genting Highlands in Malaysia. My children were stir-
crazy from being confined in the hotel room for most of the
previous day and begged to go to the amusement park attached
to the hotel, which they could see from the window. I was
fighting off a sore throat and was concerned about losing my
voice for the show that night, so I asked my friend if she would
take the children for the day. The kids were ecstatic to be able
to go play, but before they left, I reminded them that they all
had to stay together and come back before it was time to leave
for the show.

Once they had left, I tried to lie down to rest my voice, but
after about twenty minutes, I felt anxious. The kids had been
gone less than an hour, but my intuition was telling me to call

my assistant and have her bring them back. I pushed it out of my mind, knowing how disappointed they would all be to have to return to the room so soon. I returned some business e-mails and checked in with my older children on an international call. After about an hour, I still felt unsettled but couldn't understand why. Though it was still a few hours before the show, I decided to start putting on my stage makeup and fix my hair. About forty minutes later, I tried to call my assistant but couldn't get through. So I went downstairs to get something to eat and saw my sisters-in-law Michelle and Debbie with their children. I asked them if they had seen my kids. They said they hadn't. I let the feeling go for a second time and went upstairs to finish putting on my makeup; I felt it would be good to be completely ready for the show, though I had no idea why. Still, the feeling persisted that something was not right.

About thirty minutes later, my cell phone rang, displaying the assistant's number. I could feel my heart contract in my chest. I knew something was wrong before I even answered it.

She was panicked and talking very quickly. She had bought a family pass for them to go on the rides. As I found out later, they had agreed as a group that they would all take turns choosing the next ride. The day went along pretty well, but the size of the crowd in the park made the lines grow very long. It was also difficult because the rides the older kids could go on were ones that my youngest wasn't tall enough to go on. Toward the end of the day, the boys chose a roller coaster, which didn't interest the girls. My assistant stood with the two little girls as the boys waited in line and took their ride. When they were done, it was time for the girls to choose and Abi was anxious to ride the merry-go-round before they all had to return to the hotel. They were headed over to that ride when the boys announced that they wanted to purchase the photo that was taken of them on the roller coaster right at the scariest moment. The assistant told the girls they would have to wait a moment and herded the group back to the kiosk selling the photos. She got out her wallet to pay for them, and when she turned around to hand them to the boys, the girls were gone!

Thinking that they had become impatient, she and the boys started to move toward the merry-go-round, calling out my girls' names. She checked the lines for the ride and circled the entire area several times. Then she began to worry that the girls might have returned to where they had been standing near the roller coaster, and so she hurried the boys back in that direction. That was when she decided that she needed help. She called me and then alerted the first security guard she could find.

As soon as I hung up the phone, I felt sick to my stomach. Adrenaline was coursing through my body as my mind imagined every mother's horrible fear of kidnapping and worse. It was especially overwhelming because it was a foreign country where I didn't know the area at all or even speak the language. I called my brother Merrill, who was already en route to the theater to help with a sound check. I told him to get the rest of the brothers and to please start praying.

When I arrived at the amusement park, security had notified other officers in the park that the little girls were missing. We all searched as many of the areas behind the rides and down each side alley as we could, anywhere that might be over-looked. As I ran, scanning the crowds, and calling out the girls' names, I prayed for forgiveness for ignoring my intuition. I knew that I had been sent a message more than once that would have given me the chance to avoid this terrifying scenario. But that didn't matter now. All I wanted was to find my babies. Through my frantic tears, I fell to my knees and prayed that I would be given direction to where my little girls were.

A feeling of calmness descended over me, and I stopped in my tracks. I felt that I was somehow being magnetically drawn toward another section of the amusement park where no one had looked. This time I didn't ignore it. I went, trusting that there must be a reason. Just then, a security guard ran up to us, saying that the little girls had been found safe in this other sec-tion. It was down an escalator and a ways from where they had left my assistant's side. I ran there with security and saw my two darling daughters holding hands with an approaching se-curity guard. When they saw me, they both burst into tears, partly from relief and mostly because they knew how wrong it had been for them to sneak away. They explained that they thought they wouldn't have a chance to ride their ride before they had to leave, so they had wandered off on their own and gotten lost. After I was done ferociously hugging them, I in-formed them that they were grounded for the rest of their lives or until further notice and that they would have to prove to me that I could trust them again. Then reality settled in once more, and I remembered that fifteen thousand people were taking their seats to see the Osmonds onstage.

I called my brothers, who were on the verge of canceling the show if the girls weren't found. I had only ten minutes to get to the theater before the start of the show, and fortunately I knew I would make it. Even though I had ignored my intuition about calling for the children to come back to the hotel, I had for some reason followed an impulse to put all of my makeup on and have my hair finished early. If I hadn't, it would have been impossible to walk out onstage on time. I couldn't ignore the grace I had been granted from God to have my children found safe and sound and also to not let down all the people who had come to see the one and only show we were performing in Malaysia.

Over the more recent years, I've learned to listen to and trust my intuition more and more, for both large and small matters. I might have a hundred things on my list but suddenly feel the need to call a friend. More times than I can count, I call them right when they seem to need a friend the most, even though I wasn't aware of what was going on. Even with strangers, I have found I will have an intuitive feeling that I need to help someone or connect someone with a needed resource.

Probably my favorite moment of listening to my intuition happened one night at a "Meet 'n Greet" after the Las Vegas show.

A woman named Kelly introduced herself and asked if I remembered her. I laughed and said of course I did. I had gotten to know her the best when I was seventeen years old and taking a few classes at Brigham Young University in Utah. But my brothers and I had first met her and her family when we used her parents' home as the setting for a commercial shoot for a

Japanese soft drink called Calpis. She and I began to talk as if no time had passed between us. Then she introduced me to her daughter, who was with a young man I assumed she was dating. As I talked to the daughter, I couldn't stop thinking about my oldest son, Stephen. I somehow knew this was the woman for him. I tried to refrain from saying anything, because it certainly wasn't an appropriate time to bring that up. When the date stepped away for a minute, though, I asked Kelly's daughter, "How serious are you two?" She smiled and told me she was trying to decide. Being way too blunt, I told her, "Lose him. You have to meet my son." Her eyes widened at the boldness of my statement, but she laughed and said, "Sure. I'll meet him," which made me like her even more.

As it turned out, Kelly and her family were vacationing for a few days in Vegas, and they were going to be boating the next day on Lake Mead. They asked me if Stephen would like to join them. I said absolutely, as only an obnoxious mother would do!

As I was driving home, I called Stephen to tell him about my encounter and his invitation. He groaned at the thought of another blind date, especially one set up by his mother, but he agreed to go. I felt like the momentum had started, and I somehow knew this was the right thing to do.

The next afternoon, as I was driving my daughter to a dance class, my cell rang. It was Stephen. He was calling from the dock on Lake Mead. He told me, "Mom, she's so smart and funny. And, oh, by the way, you could have told me that she's gorgeous, too!"

A year and four months later, "gorgeous" Claire married my very happy son, Stephen Craig. They were meant for each other: They strengthen, challenge, entertain, and uplift each other.

Steve and I couldn't love our daughter-in-law more. She is a jewel . . . a treasure. My children adore her, as well, and our extended family has increased substantially as we now vacation and celebrate many holidays with her parents and sister.

I laughingly take credit for getting Claire and Stephen together, but I know it wasn't really me. It was simply listening to my intuition and following through on the direction that was given me. When a mother's intuition calls . . . a mother must listen!

Like my mother, I have the word "prayer" at the top of my to-do list and also at the bottom of that list every day. Even if it means I only get to sleep for a couple of hours, I still begin and end my day with prayer, reading, and meditation. It brings my spirit back into focus. It reminds me of what is important. Today, so much more is out of our hands than when my mother raised us. Life has become faster-paced, with more information available than ever before. But what I understand more fully now is that information isn't always knowledge; it can't give a woman the wisdom she seeks. Wisdom can only come from a deeper understanding of spiritual truths and values and knowing what your purpose is as a woman, a daughter, a sister, an aunt, a wife, and especially a mother. You can't "hear" that voice of intuition if your phone is beeping with another text message alert, or if you're trying to send an e-mail and schedule an appointment at the same time, or if you never have a moment alone to dream, imagine, create, and problem solve.

We have to be careful we don't let it get to the point where, like the runaway cow, we have to struggle up a rocky slope for one small patch of solitude and peace. Give it to yourself first, so that, like my mother, you have a supply to give to others. You need time to be present, to listen. It's one of the best things I think we can teach to our children, too.

Recently, I came home after doing a show. It was midnight, and I had been admiring the full moon on my drive home. As I walked through the house to make sure the kids were all tucked in, I saw a light on in Brianna's bedroom. She told me that she was having a hard time sleeping. Sometimes, my kids try to "work it" so they can stay up later or have me tell them stories and talk. If I'm tired, I tell them the story my mother used to tell me when it was late and she was tired and wanted me to go to sleep.

She would say, "I had a little doll. I hung her on the wall. I guess that's all. Good night." Then she would tuck me in, we would both giggle, she would switch off the light, and I would drift off to sleep.

My kids know that the light is going off when I start the "doll" story. I almost told it to Brianna, but the voice of my intuition told me that she needed more from her mother. She was fourteen and had just started learning to drive. I walked to the edge of her bed and whispered, "Hurry and put your shoes on. It's time for a driving lesson." Her face lit up, and two minutes later, we were both in the car with her at the wheel.

The neighborhood I live in has very wide, modern streets, and some of them end near the top of the ridge, where they are still developing new homes. There wasn't another car on the street, so I let Brianna practice driving up and down for a while.

Then I had her drive to the top, where the street ended, and there is the best view of most of Las Vegas. We sat in the car, and I listened as my daughter talked to me about anything and everything she wanted to, whatever was on her mind and in her heart. I listened to the happiness, the expectations, and the trials of being a fourteen-year-old girl today. She has worries that I never had at her age and she also has great opportunities that I didn't have, all of which feels like a lot to navigate when you're just starting to have more independence.

From our vantage point at the top of the hill, you could see the entire Las Vegas strip, which was lighting up the sky along the horizon. It's an impressive sight, but not when it's put into perspective.

I said to my daughter, "Look how beautiful the lights of the city are. It's a city that man built. But to God, it's like little children building with Lincoln Logs. Now, roll down your window and look up at the sky, at the full moon and the stars. That is God's creation and it goes on and on, many stars and galaxies beyond our human vision, all in 'apple pie order,' as my grandma would say. We have to remember that as human beings, we have certain powers. We can use our free will to do harm or to heal. We can stop a heart, but we can't start it beating in the womb when a new life is created. That's God. And I know God created you for a reason. He loves you and wants to listen to you and provide peace. I'm always here, too, to help you figure life out."

Just then, my phone beeped as it downloaded an e-mail. Brianna looked over at me and said, "Hey, Mom, can I see your phone for a minute?" I started to laugh, remembering our car ride many years ago, and so did she. I could tell by her expression that it might go out the window and over the edge of the ridge. I turned the phone off. I reached over and squeezed her hand three times. She smiled, and we leaned back to gaze up at the stars. She talked. I listened.

Knowledge

Understanding gained through experience, insight, and study.

*T*HE KEY IS LOVE

My parents at the celebration of their fortieth anniversary and a life of love.

I was in Los Angeles recently when I had a simple and profound epiphany. It was more of a "remembering" than an "aha" moment. I had flown in the night before, by myself, for an early morning press tour for the *Donny & Marie Christmas Show* at the Pantages Theatre. It was late, and I was in my hotel room writing in my journal after talking on the phone to my kids, Steve, and then my daughter who lives in Utah. Tourists from all around the world were still meandering along the Hollywood sidewalks far below my window, stopping to take photos next to the stars' names along the Walk of Fame. Down the street a couple of blocks, two mega spotlights sliced the night sky back and forth, signaling another tourist attraction. Nearby, dozens of people milled about the courtyard of the famous Grauman's Chinese Theatre, comparing the size of their own hands to the cement handprints of the stars. My life is blessed, busy, and full. I have a huge extended family, many new and old friends. But for a brief moment, as I looked out the window, I experienced how it felt to be very alone in this city of "broken dreams," one person in a city of four million residents and countless tourists who had come looking to be entertained and energized by the excitement or to escape their daily stress. As I went back to my journal, I rather unconsciously wrote a phrase that my mother lived by: "The key to life is love." In my aloneness, as I contemplated this simple truth, it gave me pause.

For most of her life, my mother wore a bracelet with a small bejeweled key charm on it. She wore it as a reminder of her belief that the key to life is love.

She must have said this to me hundreds of times when I was growing up, but it wasn't easy to absorb as a young girl. The values of our society would have us believe that the key to life is accumulating wealth, living in the best place, having a fast car, obtaining an Ivy League education, climbing the ladder to a top job title, being physically fit and beautiful and having a wardrobe envied by others, finding a handsome spouse, and having brilliant children who will also grow up to have a life that represents all of these things. Oh, and try to accomplish it all at a young age as proof of how smart you are.

However, no matter what efforts we make to build up our lives, we are each alone, despite our efforts to prove we aren't. We were designed that way: one body, one brain, one nervous system, and one heart. We're born alone, and we die alone. As far as our existence goes, we might wonder, "What's the point?" Is it to just gather what we can for ourselves until we run out of time?

If all I had to believe in was the harsh visible reality of this struggling world, it would be tough for me to find a purpose for all of it. But something tells me that we human beings wouldn't have stuck around for all these years if it were only about merely existing.

We aren't just flesh and bones; we have a deeper existence, a purpose. It's called love. If neuroscientists can't pinpoint what creates the feeling of love in the body, then it seems to me that love must have its own source of creation. I call that God. And to me, God is love.

I believe love truly is the power that unlocks the door to everything. Love is the key. The rest is meaningless without it.

My mother had very little of what society would label "success." She never graduated from college, she wore clothes she made herself, she had to relocate many, many times in her life, and she didn't drive nice cars, go to spas, or have a safe full of precious jewelry.

Yet she had an undeniable wealth of character. My mother didn't need a job title to feel worthy. She had self-worth, self-love, which first came from her trust in God.

She loved herself enough to make wise choices, which helped her to strive to live in light and in truth.

She had no codependency issues with anyone, including my father. She didn't facilitate anyone's weaknesses. She held each of us to a high standard, and we did our best to live up to her expectations.

She had her priorities in order. Her highest goal was always love, and she projected that to everyone she met, but mostly she gifted her nine children by being an example of unconditional love for us and my father.

My mother met my father in 1944 when he was newly discharged from the army. World War II was still in progress, and my mother was working as an efficiency clerk in the army's general depot in Ogden, Utah. On their first date, they went to eat chow mein (my mother's first taste of Chinese food) and then to an Abbott and Costello movie. The movie featured a song called "My Dreams Are Getting Better All the Time," and she and my father picked up the words and harmonized together quickly a cappella as soon as they left the theater. They then went to hear Tommy Dorsey's big band and danced on the patio under the stars. By the end of the evening, they were both smitten.

However, my father had to work so many jobs to support himself that my mother didn't get to see him very often. My mother wrote this story in her journal describing their relationship: *"Occasionally, he would stop by when he was driving a taxi and sing a song or two as I played piano. Chills went up and down my spine hearing his voice. It was so beautiful and mellow. We went to a movie now and then and one night he told me that I was what he had been looking for. He said he wanted to marry me but he didn't have enough money in the bank or a good enough job to take the responsibility, yet. I was totally in love. I didn't care if he didn't have any money."*

Love was the currency they started their marriage with, and love was the abundance that sustained their sixty years together. In the most difficult or trying passages of our lives, my parents always sang together and laughed together. The sound that comforted me the most as a little girl lying in bed at night was hearing my parents together in the living room, reading jokes or funny poems to each other and laughing and laughing. They taught me that love is supposed to be joyful, and if it isn't, then it's not a relationship that can hold on through the tough times. When my family did go through difficult and exhausting times, my parents would always find a way to bring light and hope to the situation.

In May of 1975, we were in the middle of a three-month tour. We had just left Mexico, where each of us had taken a turn being sick. My mother had fallen down some steps and hurt her knees, and everyone was feeling jet-lagged and over-worked by the time we reached Paris, France. My mother wrote in her journal:

"George and I had our daily checker game early this morning. He beat me as usual, so I threw a wet washcloth at him. He threw it back. That went on for a while. We laughed until we could hardly move. George was trying to get dressed but I had tied the legs of his pants in knots and stuffed his pockets with granola. He dumped my purse on the bed and mixed the contents with the granola. Jay was in our room and was laughing. Merrill heard the commotion, came over, and was laughing, too. I guess if we couldn't have a little fun, we'd go berserk. Or, maybe it's already happened. Ha!"

Like mother, like daughter. I can't resist a good food fight with the love of my life. I had made a seven-layer Jell-O salad, one that the kids love because of the rainbow of colors. While we were putting away the leftovers, I took a handful and gave

Steve a surprise facial. He jumped up from his chair and grabbed some Jell-O from the pan and chased me around the dining table to return the favor. My kids sat wide-eyed, watching us play and laugh. It wasn't something they were used to seeing while they were growing up before Steve and I got back together, but I could see by their faces that they loved the idea of their parents acting unpredictable for a couple of minutes. The next night, my son Brandon said to Steve, "Watch out, Dad. Mom made potato salad tonight."

My parents individually brought new ideas into their marriage to keep it fresh. Mother thought they should both learn Spanish as she knew it was *the language of the future in the world,*" so they bought an audio course in 1984 and started to practice daily. My father built my mother desks and workstations for all of her various sewing and craft projects. He loved to bring home new foods to try. They drank soy milk hot chocolate long before most Americans had only heard the word "soy" with sauce. They would both go to the public library, where Mom would check out books and Dad would check out movies on video, and then they would compare notes on whatever they had learned. My mother wrote and bound cookbooks and got my father to sell them at the family's Branson, Missouri, theater. They always had a new project, idea, or discovery that would capture their imaginations and send them off to research the possibilities.

My mother even had what she laughingly called her secret "backup plan" to keep my father interested. She had the habit of tucking small items she didn't want to lose into the cleavage of her chest. (Again, like mother, like daughter: It's a habit I've inherited.) She called it her "chest of drawers." Mother told me, later in life, that if she ever felt overlooked, all she had to do was tuck the television remote into her "chest of drawers," and before long, Father would come find her.

By the beginning of 1982, all nine of us had grown up and moved away. My parents' responsibility to raise, protect, and watch over their children in their home was over. I know quite a few marriages that have fallen apart once the children were grown and gone, mostly because the devotion was to the children and not to each other. When I was a single mother for four years, I could empathize with women who faced the challenge of maintaining the role of parent. It's tempting to let your children become your whole life and relinquish the idea of having an adult relationship, especially when the one you left was damaging for you emotionally. When you don't have a partner in your life, it's easy to bond more tightly with your children. But it also puts more pressure on them. At one point, one of my grown children was worried about leaving home out of concern that I might not be okay on my own. I can understand how women might feel that they are only trying to fill in the gap for both parents in their children's lives, but the children often interpret it as "My mother really needs me." With the divorce rate at 50 percent now, the chances of children feeling this type of pressure are probably even greater.

We knew as children that our parents' devotion was always to each other, first and foremost. As they aged, their relationship grew even stronger.

This is from a letter that my father wrote my mother on December 1, 1981:

"I am sure you are aware of it, but as a reminder, I state that this is our 37th anniversary of our marriage . . . of being together. 37 years of exciting, busy, happy hours all jammed into time. We could glance back on worry, stress, expectation and doubt, but why? Let's take an eager look forward and hope that the Lord will permit us to continue on with our same bag of tricks: To stay close to our children and their loved ones, to maintain good health, to influence the lives of others for good, to be close to God and feel His love, and to know and enjoy our love for each other. You have helped me enjoy the simple things in this life, things such as: your warm smile, your acts of kindness, your positive outlook on life, your never-ending desire to teach and learn . . . I am sure you are an inspired person as you always come up with so many wonderful ideas. I feel a warmth in my heart every time I see you, my dear Olive Osmond, or even if I am in a place where you have been. . . . I love you so much. The only thing I do know is that it's bigger than space."

Their depth of love and commitment to each other is the reason I married my husband, Steve, in 1982 and the reason I married him again in 2011. Curious people have asked me in the last two years how I found the trust to marry Steve again, especially since I had had so much heartbreak as a young woman when we separated the first time. This is my answer: I had the example of true love from my parents. I know that a healthy marriage can weather all types of change because of my parents' example. I know that for all of their differences, my parents shared the one thing that mattered most: values.

My parents valued God first, then each other, and then family, in that order. As children, my brothers and I understood that we were created by love and were loved "bigger than space" as well, but that we were under the stewardship of our parents, not the other way around. We didn't run their lives; they guided ours.

Steve and I share the same values. We value our God, each other, and our family, and my sweet husband loves the children, who now all call him "Dad," in a way that is "bigger than space." In so many ways, it's as if we've never been apart.

My children understand, honor, and respect Steve's and my relationship. I know I have an equal partnership built on the same respect and devotion my parents had for each other. And we have a mandatory kid-free date night every Friday to make sure we always make time for each other.

I look forward to being with my husband when life gets a little slower, and I'm excited at the possibility of feeling that fulfillment of love my mother wrote about in April of 1991:

"We spent some time with each member of our family and of course these times are the highlights of our lives. Our children all want us to stay with them and they do special little things for us to make us happy. What joy we have in our lives now, with our big family. As we grow older it seems that each day brings more and more blessings and we become more humble and appreciative for each and every one of them."

An appreciation for the simple but fine things in life was

another aspect of love as "the key" to a good life that was mir-
rored to us by our parents. They encouraged us to surround
ourselves only with people and possessions that were uplifting
to our spirits.

My parents always said, "People are always saying 'I'll be
happy when . . .' There will always be something better than
what you have. What's important is to be happy and love what
you have now."

When I was about six years old, my mother bought a blue
lead-crystal vase while we were on tour in Sweden. She kept it
on the fireplace mantel wherever we lived. It was symbolic of
one of her favorite stories, which she told us many times, and
I have repeated it to my own children often.

This is the blue vase story, copied from my mother's journal:

*A shop owner in a small town noticed a certain man that
would stop and admire the lovely blue vase in his store window each day as he went to work and as he came home. The
man wore overalls and carried a lunch bucket, so the shop
owner supposed that he worked at the local factory like many
others who lived in the area.*

*Day after day the same thing happened. Then, one day, the
man came into the store and purchased the blue vase.*

*"Sir," the owner said, "forgive my curiosity, but I've
watched you admiring this blue vase for a long time. What
made you buy it today?"*

*The man said, "Well, I live alone in a small house. I'm not
wealthy, but I value my life. I don't think material things are
all that important and yet, we are influenced and inspired if
our surroundings are neat, clean, and lovely.*

"I have only two paintings on my walls, but they are beautiful.

"My books are the best. They are uplifting and inspiring.

"I only listen to great music.

"I eat the best foods, fresh and wholesome.

"I choose my friends from the best people I meet, because they, too, influence my life.

"In other words, I want the best of everything that is possible in my life.

"This blue vase just seems to be symbolic of those things. I'm going to put it on my fireplace mantel to remind me often to seek only the best that life has to offer."

As he walked out of the store, the shop owner began to analyze his own life . . . and what could use a few changes for improvement.

Some of the most loving, unforgettable gestures of kindness in my life were simple but fine gifts. A few of these gifts have been given to me by strangers who became like angelic messengers when I needed them the most. This is one experience:

About two years after my mother passed away, I was in a fabric store picking out materials to make outfits as samples for my designer dolls. It had been a rough week, with a lot of decisions needing to be made both personally and professionally. It was still difficult for me to be in a fabric store, because it made me miss my mother more than ever. She simply buzzed with happiness whenever she was meandering around the aisles of fabrics, studying all the new materials and patterns like works of art. There was an older woman who reminded me of my grandmother shopping that day. I struck up a conversation with her in the checkout line about sewing and crafting, and eventually we began talking about canning fruits and vegetables. The way her eyes lit up when she spoke about each of her projects made me miss my mother deeply.

I told her that one of my great heartaches was that all of my grandmother's handwritten recipes for pickled beets, mustard relish, and especially the bread 'n' butter pickles she would make every year had been lost in my house fire before I could get them scanned into my computer. The woman clapped her hands together with joy and then took my arm. She told me that she had most of those recipes and offered to send them to me. It was such a warm moment and kind gesture. I was thrilled to give her my home address since she didn't have e-mail.

Two days later, I arrived home to a basket on my front porch. It was loaded with pint-size mason jars of vegetables in all varieties. Each was wrapped beautifully in tissue paper with a ribbon around the top. Attached to each ribbon was a recipe card for the type of pickled vegetable or relish in that jar. I couldn't have been more moved by her thoughtfulness. It was almost as if I had crossed paths with her to be reminded that we are being watched over by those we have loved and who have gone on.

To show her my appreciation, I sent some of my designer dolls to her home. One doll was a porcelain angel, which is what this woman was to me.

I know that my mother would tell me not to waste a minute missing her.

When she could no longer walk or move on her own, she

jotted a note to me one afternoon as I sat next to her bed. *"I can serve you better from the other side now. I will always be near."* I know she is. I sense her presence with me almost every day.

My mother would have told me: "The key is love . . . and that means loving the season of life you are in. When you are young, enjoy your youth, your education, and interacting with many different people. When you find a spouse, love your marriage and your children. Capture in your heart the moments your children are young, for they quickly pass by. In the fall of your life, appreciate your wisdom, speak your mind, and give back to the community. And in your winter season, cherish your loved ones, rest in a job well-done, love the simple pleasures of life." My mother would tell me: "Don't miss the present moment by living in the past or anticipating the future. Find a way to give and receive love right now, in the current circumstances of your life. Measure your accomplishments in love."

One night, late after a show, my daughter Rachael, who was twenty at the time, came into my room and sat on my bed to talk to me. She was at a point where she was striving to find purpose in her life that she knew was her own. She has so many talents: singing, dancing, playing instruments, creating visual arts, and designing clothing. She is easily as talented as any Osmond and could have a performing career. However, she had a different point of view to tell me about that night. She took a framed photo from my dresser of my mother and father, her grandma and grandpa, in her hands. She said, "I'm interested in so many different things. Like you, Mom. I look at your résumé and everything you've done, and I know that your talents and versatility have touched millions of people. But you always tell me that your greatest heartbreak is that you couldn't be a full-time stay-at-home mother, which is what you always wanted to be. Grandma was brilliant. She gave up having an impressive work résumé to be a full-time mother. To me, Grandma chose the higher calling, by raising nine outstanding children. Because of her sacrifice, look at what all of you, her children, have done to bring joy to the world.

"I know if I worked really hard, I could probably do anything I put my heart and soul into professionally, like you have done. I love and respect you so much because you've had to provide for our family. But if it's up to me, when the time comes, I'm not going to choose to work like you. I want my life to be like Grandma's. I want my job title to be Mother."

I shed a tear as I hugged my daughter. She has chosen the highest calling on the earth.

A woman's love nurtures the world. To be a mother takes passion, commitment, energy, sacrifice, intuition, sensitivity, intelligence, focus, and endless amounts of love. Every woman holds the key.

In 2003, as my mother lay ill in her bed, I began to ask her questions about her life, and I wrote down her answers. This is what she said about marriage and family. *"You must work for everything of value in life. If you want a college degree, you've got to put in the time, the study, the work. Your degree will not be handed to you the first day you walk into class.*

Marriage and children are the same. Family must be fought for, sacrificed for, held up and recognized as the most precious reward given to mankind."

One afternoon, about six months later, when my mother had lost her ability to speak, my father came into the room and lay down in the bed next to my mother. He looked over at me and asked: "Doesn't your mother have the most beautiful legs in the world?" My mother scratched out a note to him saying that she wanted to stand up one more time and dance with him on those legs. With the nurses' help, I moved my mother's feet to the floor and we brought her to a standing position. My father held her up in his arms and began to sway back and forth. Then he began to sing to her, using that same beautiful voice that gave her a "chill up and down" her spine as a nineteen-year-old girl. Tears flowed down their faces. Her fragile body began to tremble and sink into his arms, but they wouldn't take their eyes off each other. Nothing was more important than that moment and remembering their first date, the beginning of sixty years of love shared together.

Love

A feeling of deep devotion and affection, connecting one heart to another.

A fresh beginning of a life of love. On our wedding day, May 4, 2011.

ACKNOWLEDGMENTS

*M*y love and gratitude go to those who *mothered* this project to maturity. They include:

My literary agent at William Morris Endeavor, Mel Berger, who continuously cheered from the bleachers until I crossed the finish line. I appreciate you so much.

Kara Welsh, publisher, and Tracy Bernstein, executive editor, at New American Library for "adopting" this baby and nurturing its full potential. You have both been a blessing.

Kim Goodwin, who gave his tender loving care to every photo in this book, just like he does for every project we do together. You're the best, Kimmie, and thank you for keeping me looking current, especially since I'm forever twenty-nine. Right?!?

My executive assistant, Lorraine Wheeler, who took notes and edited and printed and copied and pasted and then did it all again more than any mother with a year's worth of school projects! Thank you, my dear friend.

My family of business associates who provide the sturdy structure that keeps me functioning, and who "walk me to the bus stop" every day to make sure I arrive at every destination safely—my management team: Greg Sperry, Darla Sperry, and my assistant, Maggie Yahner. Also, my publicists, Alan Nierob and Allison Garman, who keep a caring eye on the report cards. I couldn't get through a day without you ALL!

As every mother knows, you have to have at least one of those great girlfriends in your life who understands you to the core, strengthens you through the shaky moments, laughs with you through the long days, loves your children as if they were hers, listens to your thoughts, adds new insights, and helps you make sense of it all. My friend and coauthor, Marcia Wilkie, knew and loved my mother, knows and loves my children and husband, and has been my sister in spirit since the day we met in 1998. This book would have never happened without her. Thank you for the long two-year labor on this baby, my Marsh! I love you with all my heart.

To those I live my life to love more and more every single day, hour, minute, and second: my beautiful children, Stephen (and his wife, Claire), Jessica, Rachael, Michael, Brandon, Brianna, Matthew, and Abigail. I could never have understood the magnitude of joy in the word "motherhood" without each one of you in my life.

And finally, to my husband, Steve, who supports and sustains me through his love and belief in me, even through my unique and sometimes crazy life. The greatest gift you give to me is your undying support of my true and chosen career, to be a mom. Thank you, my angel, for loving and parenting these children, whom I adore, and for helping to mend any and all of the broken pieces along the way. I love you to the height and depths of my heart and soul.

Marcia Wilkie would like to offer her deep appreciation to

Mel Berger of William Morris Endeavor, Tracy Bernstein of New American Library, Patricia Bechdolt and Teresa Fischer, for being there throughout. And a full-hearted thank-you to Marie Osmond. ("She shall rejoice in time to come. She openeth her mouth with wisdom; and in her tongue is the law of kindness." Proverbs 31: 25–26)